Set Apart
and Chosen

*God uses ordinary women
to do extraordinary things*

*Listen for God's voice,
then walk in His path!*

Isaiah 30:21

Tony Wylie

EDITED BY
Kimmoly K. LaBoo

Introduction

"For you are a people holy to the LORD your God.
Out of all the peoples on the face of the earth,
the LORD has chosen you to be his treasured possession."
Deuteronomy 14:2

The Word of God declares, "For many are called, but few are chosen.", Matthew 22:14. Many people hear the call of God, but few will respond because they are the ones who are truly hearing. Twenty extraordinary women have come together to answer the call, sharing their wisdom, pain, joy, and faith. Their trials have been the springboard of their true callings. The testimonies of their pain are the joy, deliverance and healing of others.

Set Apart and Chosen, those were the words God spoke to me at 2:30AM one morning. I woke out of my sleep, sat up on my bed and asked, what do you want me to do with that Lord? He quickly revealed that I was to gather a group of extraordinary, humble, women that are impacting the world with their gifts and talents to help other women find the extraordinary within themselves.

My prayer for you, is that you find strength, healing, faith and courage, through the stories in these pages. May they uplift and edify you.

You are beautiful, you are brilliant, you are Extraordinary. Walk boldly in the gifts and calling that God has placed on your life.

· ·

Isaiah 26:3-4

You will keep in perfect peace

those whose minds are steadfast,

because they trust in you.

Trust in the LORD forever,

for the LORD, the LORD himself,

is the Rock eternal.

· ·

 **LaVerne Day** is retired after dedicating 31 years of faithful service to the citizens of Maryland at Crownsville Hospital Center, as a Direct Care Assistant. She treated all her patients with dignity and respect. She worked in the Adolescent, Alcoholic, and Adult Psych units. When Crownsville Hospital Center closed its doors in 2004, LaVerne moved to Spring Grove Hospital where she dedicated three years of State service. She also worked for the United Cerebral Palsy Association. She is the loving mother to a son, R.C., and daughter, Kimmoly.

Beyond the Shadows

By LaVerne Day

Years ago, when I was in school, I was bullied and called names that I don't care to remember. I held everything in like it did not bother me. I felt that being loved by men was my only way out. I thought sex and feeling loved was what it would take to make me feel better about myself. I went on with my life that way. I met men that I should not have been with. I often felt like I would have to pay for my mistakes.

I didn't feel good about myself. I felt if I had a good-looking man, the attention would be off me and focused on him being with me. My self-esteem was not good at all. It all stemmed from my school-day experiences. My siblings acted like they hardly knew me. I think they wanted to distance themselves from me because of the names I was called. I never felt beautiful, even as I got older. I didn't feel that I was good enough because none of the attention was focused on me.

I graduated high school in 1966. I met Mr. LaBoo after graduation and I was on top of the world. I was working as a dishwasher in Severna Park at Reads, and he was helping with construction to build the Bay Bridge. I would always meet him there. Back then, I was wearing Cinnamon pantyhose and he loved them. He asked me to marry him, but I said no because I felt like I was not up to his family's standards. I was a little old country girl. He was from the other side of the tracks. I became pregnant in 1969 with our beautiful little girl, the love of my life, my pride and joy. She was 6 pounds, 9 ounces. She was a very healthy baby girl. We named her Kimmoly LaBoo. He was so proud of his little girl. My aunt gave her the nickname Munchie because she had the prettiest little cheeks. Mr. LaBoo and I eventually went our separate ways.

Seven years later, after meeting my son's father, I became pregnant again. January 7, 1976 was a day I will never forget. Still today a dark cloud hangs over my head because I don't know what happened to my son. I had a very difficult delivery, which left him unable to breathe. I never got to see my baby. The nurse came in to tell me that he was flown to University Hospital because he had a breathing problem. They told me that I could not hold him until after I got out of the hospital. Then a few hours later, I got a call saying my baby had died. I asked if they could hold him there until I got out of the hospital so that I could see him and they said no.

I will never forget that pain until the day I die. My sister and her husband were the only ones to see him. I asked her if she could take a picture of him, but she was not able to. I don't even know what he looked like. I was devastated but I suppressed it all. It's the most traumatic hurt I've endured. I lost my son. To come from a hospital listening to sounds from the other babies and to leave without your own is devastating. To come home to baby items and a crib was heartbreaking. The only memory I have is a birth certificate, not even a death certificate. It was so painful. Blocking it out was how I coped.

I had to hide the hurt and pain from my daughter and I didn't know what she was going through. We never talked about how she was feeling, but through it all she was such a good girl.

A year later I was pregnant again. I had another baby, hoping to make up for the one I'd lost. I had another difficult preg-nancy, a breech birth in which the baby had to be turned. It was a full-term pregnancy but the turning left him with severe brain damage. I never knew it until he was three years old. He wasn't saying words and he was not feeding himself. The doctor sent us to Kennedy Krieger Institute for an evaluation. That's when I found out that he had severe brain damage and he would never talk. That is heartbreaking news for a parent to hear. The only words he ever spoke were "Kim", repeatedly, and the word "Stop."

He did not know how to do sign language so he had to learn to follow verbal directions. After accepting that news, I was told by the doctor he had scoliosis and that he was curving the wrong way and if he did not get surgery he would be bent over the rest of his life. His vertebrae had to be broken and reset. It was a very dangerous surgery. After the surgery I got a hospital bed at home because he had to be log-rolled. He had to wear a plastic roll around his waist to stop him from bending while he healed. He would hold on to the bed for me to change and bathe him. It was summer time and as fast as I would change him, he would be wet again. The plastic was very hot and made him sweaty. I also had to get an aide to be with him at night because I worked the night shift at the hospital. God brought him through it all. Before the surgery he was almost toilet trained. However, the surgery stopped him from being able to be toilet trained. He never was able to grasp the full concept. I prayed so hard for that to happen, but it wasn't in God's plan. His surgery did make him taller, and then all he liked to do was run.

At one point, R.C. had bacteria in his blood and had to be rushed to the hospital right away. I was told the medication they first put him on wasn't working. I had to have faith that he was going to be okay. He looked up at me, as sick as he was, and just then the doctor walked in and said they had begun trying another medication and it was working. I said, "Thank God." I knew God was with him. I was not afraid at all.

God has truly been a blessing to me in so many ways. He put an angel by my side, which was my sister. She has been there for him every step of the way. She was at every meeting and wrote letters, helping to fight for him. Without her and God, I don't know how I would have made it.

There was a training program at Grafton School that was supposed to help him. It was in Berryville, Virginia. The pain and hurt I felt when I had to leave him there was indescribable. I was not able to call him or visit him for a whole month in order for him to get adjusted to the new surroundings. My heart hurt so badly when I had to leave him. He stood looking out of the window like, "Mom, why are you leaving me here?" I cried for days. It was like something was ripped away from me. I had to suppress all my feelings and hold them inside. I acted like it did not bother me. I did not want my daughter to know how much I was hurting inside. She hadn't the slightest idea of how deep the pain was. I knew she felt like all the attention went to him. I was doing the best that I could do. Her silence let me know it was just as hard for her to deal with.

For a month every weekend we made that two-and-a-half-hour drive to Berryville, Virginia, after I had worked the night shift, until he was released. I would be so sleepy, but I still made the trip. That's what a caring mother who loves her child does.

After that, I kept him home for as long as I could, then I learned that he had behavior problems. He was self-injurious, biting his hand. He began going to Central Special School and then Marley Glen Special School. After several meetings it was decided that he had to be placed in a 24-hour supervision, Residential placement. There is not a day that goes by that I don't worry about my son. I give all the support I can as a mother. There have been some rough roads, but I thank God we made it through. He is now 41 years old and I still work hard to see that he is safe and taken care of properly. I am his voice. I must speak for him.

I am learning so much more about my son. He loves nature. He likes to feel the wind blowing on his face. He gets a big smile on his face when he feels the wind. He loves to hear birds tweeting and he loves music, especially the oldies but goodies. He loves to smile.

I thank my sister Geraldine for her support, she taught me how to deal with certain situations where my son was concerned. The workers at Providence Center for the great job they are doing with him and Langston Green for caring for my son. It has not been easy; it takes special people to work with special needs adults and children. I thank Ms. Estelle for doing such a great job with my son. She was like a mother to him and he loved her so much. Thanks to all the staff that have cared for him.

As I think back over my life, it's hard to know what God was telling me when I was young. The message I felt like God was giving me was He took the first child to wake me up and I did not listen, so He said, I will give you another that will not talk. I couldn't see the outcome of it all until I looked back over my life. I love my son dearly. I will fight for him until the day I die because of his disability.

The pain of losing my first son never healed but I went on with life and made the best of the situation. My grandmother said, "You make your bed hard and you lie hard," and I did...but the joy of my two children has kept me here. I am so proud of them both. I would not change the hand that God dealt me at all. I feel like I made all the wrong decisions for all the right reasons because God has blessed me beyond my wildest dreams.

My daughter and son have given me joy but there is still something lacking in my life.

I feel like I am soul searching. The loss of a child keeps you wondering why, what, when, and where? What happened, why it happened, when does it all end and, where is he in heaven?

As a mother I have shed many tears in silence, but I found that tears were not getting me anywhere. I had to dry my tears and go on and deal with the situation at hand. It took 40 years before I could even talk about this pain that runs deep inside my soul. Blocking the pain out was my coping skill, until my daughter encouraged me to write about it. I love my daughter very much; she is a gift that God has blessed me with. I am finally living beyond the shadows.

Isaiah 41:10

So do not fear, for I am with you;
do not be dismayed, for I am your
God. I will strengthen you and
help you; I will uphold you with
my righteous right hand.

Kimmoly K. LaBoo is a Published Author, International Speaker and Certified Life Coach. She is at the helm of LaBoo Publishing Enterprise, as CEO and founder. She is a highly respected change agent in her community and around the world.

Her award-winning company was created for the independent self-publisher. Kimmoly enjoys providing expert guidance and unlimited support to her clients, helping them recognize their brilliance, sharing their stories with the world, as writers.

She has dedicated her life to serving girls and women through mentoring, and coaching. Her compassionate coaching style, challenges clients to embrace change and show up confidently, using their unique gifts and talents to impact and serve others.

She was recently named among the Top 25 Women in Business by Courageous Woman magazine. She has appeared on Think Tech Hawaii, WPB Networks, Heaven 600 Radio, ABC2News, FOX5 News, and has graced many stages speaking and training to include, Department of Veterans Affairs, Blacks in Government National Training Conference, and Coppin State University.

Kimmoly is the mother of two amazing son's and currently resides in Honolulu, Hawai'i.

Things Remembered
By Kimmoly K. LaBoo

I wasn't popular, I wasn't pretty, I wasn't proud. I just wasn't that girl. Growing up for the first eight years of my life as the only child of a single-parent mom, I know I was spoiled rotten. However, I don't look back on my childhood and think, *Oh, I had so much fun*. I remember being well dressed as a little girl, white tights, cute dresses, two big bush balls on each side of my head. My mom took pride in my appearance and made sure I was in church every Sunday. My cousins and I always looked sharp.

I remember waiting for hours on end by the door, glancing out the window at the sound of every car door closing, hoping it was my daddy coming to visit me. Often, my hopes were smashed, like a glass shattering against a brick wall. Although he did show up one time, around Christmas, with a gift. I only know that because I have a picture to prove it. It's the only photo I have of me as a child with my dad. I was sitting on his lap, smiling from ear to ear.

I remember a man jumping off the balcony of Allen's Apartments because he was drunk and in love with my mom, but she didn't want to date him anymore. That is such a vivid memory for me. I recall peeking through the slotted guardrails from the second floor, staring at him lying face down in a pool of blood. I remember my mom yelling for someone to get me in the house. I can even recall the song that was playing on the radio when I went back inside: "You Make Me Feel Brand New" by the Stylistics. Funny thing is, I think I was only three or four years old at the time.

I remember around the age of eight visiting my grandmother's house. I remember things that happened there that nobody really wants to talk about. There was a lot of stuff swept under the living room rug of Grandma's house. Decades later when I finally found the courage to uncover some of the dirt, there were others that didn't want to acknowledge it because they would have to face their own demons if they acknowledged mine. I guess the good thing is, it freed me, but unfortunately still holds them bound. I learned that just because you avoid a thing doesn't mean it doesn't exist and certainly doesn't mean it will go away. I also learned to accept the apology I never received.

Around the age of 10, I remember playing outside with my cousins, two boys and one girl in St. Georges Gate apartments in Glen Burnie, Maryland. By then I had a baby brother and an alcoholic stepdad that I never wanted to call Daddy but was forced to. I remember playing hopscotch, tennis and dodge ball in the breezeway, skate boarding, big wheeling, and catching lightning bugs and bees in glass jars with my cousins. I remember being head over heels for a boy named Brian and being forbidden by my mom to go to his house, which was just across the street. I thought it was neat because he lived in a two-story, single-family home, with two parents and an above-ground pool, just through the woods that separated the apartments from the houses on the main road. Somehow, I would find myself with my cousins sitting in Brian's kitchen eating snacks. I remember my cousin pretending, playing push and pull, as if he was going to toss me in the pool one day. I remember the moment it wasn't pretend anymore as I struggled to reach the surface of the water that covered my face. I couldn't swim. I remember how angry my mom was when she came home from work and heard how I had walked into the house dripping wet from head to toe, fully clothed. We all were punished, but theirs always lasted longer than mine, and I was great at teasing them through the little window that was just above the ground where my cousins were peeking out.

I remember moving to Annapolis, Maryland at the age of 13. My mom had finally mustered up the courage to leave my "stepdad", a term I use loosely because they were never married. We had temporarily been living with my aunt and cousins. We moved into a community that was down the street and around the corner from 4th Ward, which was full of drug dealers and users on the corner, and right next to the cemetery. Despite that I remember how happy my mom was to move into that 3-bedroom, two-story townhome. It was a step up for us. My brother and I had our own separate rooms. About that cemetery—I remember grown folks saying, "Child, it's not the dead folks you have to worry about; it's the ones that are living." My mom always planted pretty flowers in our tiny flower bed in front of the house. She even won a citation from the Governor's office one time because she always kept it looking so nice. She took so much pride in it.

Years passed, but I remember still holding out hope for my dad to come and get me. I sat on the front step with my suitcase packed. It would be the first time I would ever spend the night with my dad, my two younger sisters and their mom, my dad's wife. I remember running into the house to tell my mom he was there. I was so excited. We drove all the way to Baltimore City, where they lived. They had a house with a porch and a gated front yard. I was really excited to see my two younger sisters. It was Christmas Eve. They had a tall tree in the living room. On

Christmas morning I remember feeling 'less than'. I was happy to be with my sisters and my dad, but it was evident that they lived a life I knew nothing about. I can't even remember what my present was. All I remember was they got a new computer. I remember thinking, *Wow, is this what it's like to live with Daddy?* I really loved my youngest sister; she was funny. When she found out there wasn't any milk to eat her cereal, she poured water in it, claiming that the milk's only purpose was to get the cereal wet, so what difference did it make? I thought that was just nasty, but she ate it.

I spent most of my time caring for my baby brother while my mom was working the night shift at Crownsville Hospital to feed and clothe us. The kids in the neighborhood teased me, saying that he was probably really my son since I had him with me all the time. They were stupid. I remember my mom being upset with my dad often because he wouldn't pay child support. She said he paid just enough to keep them from throwing him in jail. I never realized how hard it must have been on my mom until I was much older. Yet I never felt like we had less than other people. She always kept our home clean and we always had food to eat. On the weekends, she would always say we had to tidy up. I swear I couldn't see what was out of place.

I had a hard time learning, so school was never fun for me. I didn't have many friends, I wasn't considered popular, and I considered girls who were in sororities to be mean. That is because they were back then. If you were not light-skinned, pretty with long, pressed hair, or dating someone from the high school sports team, you just weren't cool. I didn't like my teachers, I didn't like most of the students—I didn't like much at all. I was just an ordinary girl.

I had my share of bum boyfriends too, but that's a whole other story. Well, perhaps some of it is relevant. My high school sweetheart got another girl pregnant. Then I met a guy and ran away from home at the age of 17 because I didn't want to live by my mom's rules anymore. Looking back on it now, I think all kids at that age thought their parents' rules were insane. However, there was a lot more to it than that for me. I went to live with my boyfriend and his family on the Eastern Shore. He turned out to be a drug dealer and user and I found myself in a horrible situation. I had no business being there. My mom tried to warn me the day he, in anger, threw a glass Coke bottle at my head in her house, but I was "in love". She told me things like that didn't get better with time; they would only get worse. I didn't listen. We eventually got our own apartment, but that ended abruptly the day he tried to choke the life out of me. That was a wakeup call for me. The day it happened was the day I left him and never looked back. One thing I did learn from my mom was we don't put up with abuse.

When I graduated high school, I already had a decent job working for the Federal government, one that I only got because my Business Administration teacher, Ms. Doris Scott, forced me to take the test when I was just 16 years old. To this day, I think she was God-sent. I'm pretty sure she changed the course of my life forever with that one move.

I was married by the age of 21 and had my first child at the age of 22, the same age my mom was when she had me. That lasted for seven long, arduous years. The best thing about that marriage was my two amazing sons that came from it.

I remember the day my dad died. My uncle called me at work to break the news. I left immediately. I held my tears until I got to my car and then I broke down. I had just seen him at the hospital a few weeks earlier. He'd been recovering from triple bypass surgery. They had moved him to a rehabilitation center. It was the day after his birthday. Apparently, he was upset with the staff about something. He was very angry. Who knows what really happened, but the next call that came was the call saying he'd had a heart attack and died.

I remember going to the funeral and struggling to breathe at his burial. I couldn't believe he was gone. I couldn't bring myself to walk up to the tent where they were about to lower him into the ground. I just remembered our last conversation at the hospital and how he managed to smile when I walked into the room. He said, "There's my Kimmy Kim." He told me I looked beautiful. The little girl in me still holds on to that. I'm grateful for the relationship we were able to build in my adult years, despite his absence in my youth.

It was somewhere around the age of 28 when I discovered I had a love for children. It started with me teaching Sunday School at Asbury Town Neck Church in Severna Park, Maryland. Then I started a Bible study with a group of little boys in our neighborhood. They were my son's friends. They loved God and they wanted me to teach their friends about Him too. We formed a full-on Bible study with about seven boys around the age of 11 in my townhouse. I remember one parent asking me how I thought I was going to get little boys to want to come inside from playing to study the Bible. The funny thing was, Bible study started at 6PM, they were always on my front step at 5:50PM waiting for me to open the front door. I bought all of them brand new Bibles and I remember teaching them all 66 books of the Bible. They knew how to find each one without using Bible tabs. It was great. A couple of years later I started mentoring girls at a middle school that was associated with my job. Five years after that I started my own mentoring program for teenage girls. We first began meeting in a small conference room inside a McDonald's on Security Boulevard. I started my own business and ran that program in Baltimore County for 10 years. We had mother/ daughter retreats that were amazing. I could see how God was using the broken pieces of my life to bring healing to the lives of others. I started writing books and speaking to women and girls around the world, including Ghana, West Africa. I remember wanting to pack two little girls into my luggage to bring them home with me from that trip. Their names were Abigail and Jennifer. They were adorable.

I finally loved my life. I loved making an impact. I loved helping little girls and fatherless daughters to know their worth, I loved helping divorced women heal, I loved helping people share their stories through the gift of writing. I loved watching my own children grow and although I know I wasn't the best mom ever, they often tell me otherwise. For all these things I am grateful.

God saw me as beautiful, gifted, talented, and valuable. I just had to grow to a place through all my trials to see what He saw.

Who would have ever thought God would have used my life in such an extraordinary way? Not me—I'm just an ordinary girl that God is using to make an impact in this world.

Now, as the CEO of my own publishing company, I help people turn their dreams of becoming a published author into a reality. People are being healed through the process of writing, sharing their stories and impacting the lives of others.

Over the course of my life, there were many things along the way that tried to derail my destiny, but God had other plans. Jeremiah 29:11 says, "For I know the thoughts I think toward you, plans to prosper you, to give you a hope and a future."

What I remember now is that God loves me unconditionally.

**Lisa M. Jones** is a transformational leader, skillful coach, strategic educator, influential philanthropist, successful businesswoman, and world-renowned inspirational speaker. She is the Chief Executive Officer of Jones Jewels & Associates, where she has leveraged over 25 years of business knowledge to educate others in the area of personal development, business strategy development and financial literacy. As a result of Lisa's innovative leadership, business, and financial coaching, individuals, teams, and organizations are inspired to maximize their fullest potential, reach their financial goals, and execute their dreams.

Lisa M. Jones is dedicated to affecting and infecting people so that their lives transform from vision to reality. Lisa is an impactful change agent, whose experiences include facilitating professional learning for government agencies including, but not limited to, Voice of America, General Services Administration, Environmental Protection Agency, and Food and Drug Administration, and being the keynote speaker at over 150 leadership schools nationwide.

Lisa M. Jones' journey to greatness exemplifies that success is a "journey and not a destination." Through this journey, Lisa desires to inspire others with her walk, encourage them with her talk, and to elevate with her giving.

Living a purposeful life,
Lisa M. Jones
Jones Jewels and Associates, Inc.

Another Level
By Lisa M. Jones

**When God said this year, you will go to another level,
I had no idea it would come in the form of cancer.**

In March 1995, I made a decision that would reshape, redefine and restore my whole life. As a single parent with a six-year-old daughter, all I wanted was to make ends meet and provide a level of comfort for my little angel. I didn't make a lot of money as an administrative assistant at Johns Hopkins University and I didn't live paycheck to paycheck either; I lived paycheck to Monday. I didn't own a car and I lived with my parents in inner city Baltimore, where the income level was low and the drug transactions were high. Based on statistics, as a single African-American mom in the community where I grew up, I was supposed to be on the system, depending on the government to raise my daughter. I felt that the only way I could build the lifestyle I wanted was to go into business for myself.

John 1:46 – "Can anything good come out of Nazareth?"

Although I grew up surrounded by the chaos of the city streets, I was protected by two of the best parents a girl could ever hope to have. My siblings and I were not a product of our surroundings, but we were a product of our environment. My parents kept a spotless home that demanded order and respect. They laid a solid foundation of love, Christianity and music. We sang gospel music quite a bit and we read the Bible together as a family. At a young age, I developed an interest in the word of God and I studied his word daily. I joined a women's Bible study group where each participant was twice my age. I remember hosting a session at my home and being responsible for bringing forth the word. I chose the Parable of the Sower. It was the most powerful story to me at that time. I read it over and over and God would minister to me in ways that I felt set apart and chosen.

After high school I had to make a decision about my future. The pressure of determining my self-worth and my calling was stressful. I didn't know which direction to turn. At one point I thought I wanted to be an attorney, so I started pursuing a degree in law. After a few years of working in domestic law for the legal aid bureau, my passion for law changed. I couldn't deal with the domestic issues that the women were enduring. I then looked into corporate law and although I enjoyed a good debate, once again it didn't hold my interest. I later decided to go back to school to pursue an MBA at John Hopkins University. While at John Hopkins, a friend invited me to a business meeting. At that meeting they were discussing finances, building a business and numbers. I love, love, love numbers. I was drawn to financial literacy and servicing a family's financial needs. I was also drawn to the state licenses that I would hold. I understood that with those licenses I could dictate my income. And this is where my life, my faith, my identity and my purpose were shaped.

IN THE BEGINNING HE SAID LET THERE BE LIGHT.

It was like the lights were turned on. I had no idea what I was in store for, but it felt right. I thought I was going to help a few families, make a few extra dollars on the side and call it a day. After all, I still had my full-time job, I was a single parent and I still had no car. An extra $500 a month would make a difference in my household. The average person who files bankruptcy does so because their household is $500 short a month. I definitely fit into that category and being able to identify a solution that I could get passionate about made me pretty happy. I immediately went into a personal development frenzy. I read book after book. I studied the world of finance and I obtained all the licenses to ensure that I was compliant. I started hosting financial literacy workshops, stewardship workshops, creative financial literacy parties and so on. I had the licenses. I was creative. I had the work ethic, but because I walked through the door a woman with low self-esteem and self-doubt, I had not realized the success that I wanted to attain. I felt like a loser. My eight-year relationship had failed, my finances were a mess, my car had been repossessed and my ability to keep a roof over my head without my parents' assistance was nonexistent. I was in a low place, but I still managed to hang on to a little faith. God loved me, I just knew He did. This could not be the best he had for me. He would never set me up to fail; therefore, it had to be me. What was I doing wrong? The self-talks were negative and unproductive. It was time for a change.

In the Bible, God tells us about the tower of Babel. There was a generation of people who decided they were going to build a tower to touch the heavens. You could not convince them that this was not possible. God looked down on them and He said, look at man. Whatever man puts his mind on, it will not be denied him. The only way that God could stop them from building the tower was to change their language. This is why it's called the tower of Babel. If you don't speak the same language, it's impossible to complete a task together. God wanted me to know that first you have to put your mind on it and then you have to speak the right language. That was the defining moment that catapulted my life to another level. I became obsessed with affirmations. SPEAK WHAT YOU SEEK UNTIL YOU SEE WHAT YOU SAY. I said God, you are not a man that you should lie; you love me too much to set me up to fail. Day by day and hour by hour I walked around reciting my affirmations.

I WILL BE ON THE COVER OF MAGAZINES AND TV SCREENS. I WILL BE THE MOST SOUGHT-AFTER SPEAKER IN ALL THE WORLD. I WILL MAKE DECISIONS BASED ON MY DESIRES AND NOT BASED ON MY BANK ACCOUNT. I WON'T CHASE MONEY, MONEY WILL CHASE ME. I SERVE AN EL-SHADDAI GOD, I HAVE MORE THAN ENOUGH. I AM A MASTER RECRUITER AND A MASTER AT BUILDING RELATIONSHIPS. I ATTRACT PEOPLE WHO WANT MORE OUT OF LIFE. I AM A WINNER, A PROVIDER, THE GO-TO PERSON FOR MY FAMILY. I AM A CHANGE AGENT, AN ENCOURAGER, A LEADER OF LEADERS. I LEAD WITH INTEGRITY. MY DISCERNMENT IS HEIGHTENED AND I SEE WHAT FOLKS ARE NOT SAYING. WHEN I SIT WITH FAMILIES TRUST IS ESTABLISHED IMMEDIATELY.

This was my language throughout my day. The subconscious mind doesn't know the difference between fantasy and reality. You can train your mind to believe whatever you want. I started to believe everything I was saying. It all starts in the mind. Change your mind and you will change your bank account, your friends and your zip code. Eagles want to hang with eagles and chickens like to hang with chickens. Eagles like to soar, but chickens like to flock. I started hanging with eagles, where the standards of excellence required more of me. Increase was mandatory in all areas of my life. I learned that there were five areas of prosperity: Spiritual, Mental, Physical, Relationships/Social and Financial.

Success doesn't start or end with money. True success is in one's mindset and it was a requirement to work on all five areas.

Once I understood the requirements to gain growth, I became consumed with living a life of order and success. The more I grew mentally, the more my activity and business grew. There were naysayers around doubting my crusade, but I didn't let it stop me. All they did was fuel my eagerness to win. God started showing me what could be. I believed every message of wisdom He sent my way. His voice was more qualified, and it outweighed the naysayers. I was so excited and grateful for the possibilities. One thing I learned throughout this stage of my process was that more often than not, people were vision-rich but execution-poor. They talked a good game. They were always starting to start. They would say things like, I started to do that, but they would never actually start. When I started following my vision it bothered them because they had to look at themselves. I would tell them, stop starting to start and just start.

My process was humbling and necessary. It made me stronger and wiser. I learned how to not only recite scriptures but live by them and execute them. Throughout each year my faith in God grew, my esteem grew, and I became bulletproof. Finally, my business was moving in the right direction. What it took me a year to make in corporate America, I was making in a month. Then in a few short years, I found myself in an income bracket that only two percent of the world can claim. I didn't have to leave my house to make six figures a year. It turned out to be far greater than I could have ever imagined. I was in awe.

I delivered on the promises I had made to my daughter and parents. When I began my business, I asked them for support and time to go build. As a result of their unwavering support, I was able to retire my parents and provide a lifestyle for both them and my daughter. I am blessed to have the most amazing parents a girl could ever ask for. They are my biggest cheerleaders. During my building years, they made my task easier to bear because I knew my daughter was getting the care that she needed whenever I was away. To keep my daughter Shanina focused on the prize and not the price, we would do vision boards and we had a dream book. We wrote every bucket list item in that dream book. Once done, we would write COMPLETED next to it. It was amazing. Everything was going well.

I went from being an insecure girl who grew up in inner city Baltimore where the income level was low, but the drug transactions were high to the single mom of a six-year-old child and the girl who lived paycheck to Monday to a financially stable woman who was traveling all over the world speaking on big stages about her humble beginnings. Remember I used to say I will be on the cover of magazines and TV screens? For over 15 years, I saw those words manifest. I was featured on the cover of *Success* magazine. I was asked to start a talk show twice, one of which was with a well-known radio personality. I've done countless radio shows, and I took my opportunity to the next level. I have been booked as a keynote speaker for the federal government for Black History month, Women's History month and Economic Empowerment month. I hosted leadership workshops, trainings for multiple government agencies and I have been the featured guest speaker for leadership schools nationwide. I've spoken on conference calls worldwide, telling my From Hood to Good story. I had reached a level of financial independence. It was the most amazing ride I could have ever imagined. AND THEN...the big boom came.

Romans 8:28—"And we know that all things work together for good to those who love God, to those who are the called according to His purpose."

Every stage, conference call, workshop and coaching session I spoke, I gave God the honor, glory and praise. I made it very clear that it was my faith in God and the process that got me to the level of success I had achieved. I was the MVP of a major financial services company and my name was known worldwide. I went from never flying to traveling all over the world. And sometimes, when I arrived at the airport, limos awaited and the red carpet was rolled out. The government was paying me $3000 an hour to speak. I couldn't take the credit for the significant lifestyle change. It was all by the grace of God. God honors his word, but THE enemy had been made.

In the book of Job, Satan asked God, "Would Job worship you if he got nothing out of it? You have always protected him and his family and everything he owns. You bless everything he does, and you have given him enough cattle to fill the whole country. But now suppose you take away everything he has? He will curse you to your face."

In 2011, God said to me that this would be my year to go to another level. My mentor told me to slow down in my travel and to take that year to allow people to serve and speak for me. I thought, *OMG, this next level must mean my income is going to increase to $500,000 annually. I will open three more brokerages. LIFE IS GOOD.* I was ready for an amazing year.

I was told, Lisa you will go to another level. I had no idea that that level would come in the form of cancer. This was my Job experience.

On April 8, 2011 the nurse called to say the doctor wants to see you and he wants you to be his last patient. I knew that didn't sound right so I called my mentor, Mike Evans, to tell him about the call I received from the nurse. We prayed, and I went to the appointment as planned. I must admit that I wasn't expecting the news I received. The doctor said, "You have stage 4 cervical cancer." WHAT…How did this happen? I wasn't on medication; everything was going well. Bad timing, come on now! I was in shock. I was numb, and I remember leaving and going straight to a hotel because I didn't want anybody to see me upset. All kinds of thoughts went through my mind like, how dare this happen to me. I don't have time to entertain this issue. I have conferences to attend, agents to train and workshops to host. Also, my family needed me—remember, I retired my parents. The big "C' was in full effect. I didn't tell my family I had cancer. I hid it from everybody because talking about it was so hard. I couldn't bear hearing myself admit to that illness over and over. So I kept it to myself. Only three people knew what I was going through: my mentor Mike Evans, my cousin Andrea Jackson and my friend William Barnes. They kept my secret as I requested and with great compassion, they sowed into me daily. They knew I was undergoing serious warfare, so they spoke positive words of affirmation to me and due to the pain and suffering I was enduring I couldn't speak, so I just listened and tried to believe that what they were saying was true. It helped but as the days passed by and the illness progressed, I couldn't hear anything positive anymore.

Everything took a turn for the worse. I got so sick that I could no longer do speaking engagements. The pain was excruciating. I had stopped showing up at my office regularly. The agents were starting to see that something was wrong.

Surgery was scheduled, and I knew it was time to tell my family. I called my sister Bridgett and told her what I was dealing with and after I hung up, I realized that that wasn't a smart move. She was at work and the tears wouldn't stop flowing. I am told she had all of her co-workers crying that day. I asked Bridgett not to tell anybody just yet. How one can have so much pride at a time like this, I don't know. In my mind I was protecting them from the pain of watching another family member endure illness.

As the time grew near for surgery, I realized I had to tell not only my family but my organization too. I invited my leaders to breakfast and broke the news to them. I asked them to be strong and hold the organization together. It was time to really use the leadership skills I taught, and I knew they were capable of doing so. It's hard to watch your leadership suffer but they moved forward with the game plan as expected. Now I had to tell the family. One particular day all my siblings decided to hang out at our parents' home. I was upstairs in my room sick, but I knew I had to get it over with. I texted my sister Bridgett and asked her to tell everyone. I also asked her to tell them not to call me right now, and I didn't want to hear anybody crying. They were very obedient. I was listening intently to see if they were downstairs crying, but I didn't hear anything. It was quiet. I stayed in my room at my parents' house and attempted to sleep.

Right before surgery, it got really bad. I stopped believing that I would make it, so I put together my funeral. This way my family wouldn't have to endure the pain of planning a service. I got my affairs in order and I talked to my business partners about what I wanted to happen with my brokerage at my death. When they wheeled me into surgery, I truly didn't believe I would exit alive. Cold steel was everywhere. The anesthesiologist was the last voice I heard, and she asked what vacation I wanted to take when I got better. I said Hawaii and then I was out.

RECOVERY: When I came to, my parents and sister were standing around my bed looking at me. I asked if I was alive and they said yes. I asked them why they were crying. I was so out of it and amazed that I was alive. I spent ten days in the hospital after surgery. My daughter lived in Atlanta, GA but she came home and slept beside my bed every night. I was weak and in pain, so my daughter had to assist me with eating, going to the bathroom and bathing. It was certainly a change in roles.

I endured warfare as I still questioned why me. I never blamed God; I was trying to figure out what I did to deserve this. After being released from the hospital, I was still really sick. I would moan and cry all night. My parents would pray over me every night, and my sister Bridgett and niece Briana watched over me throughout the day. There were many times that I had to go to the emergency room because I had a high fever or unbearable pain. The doctor had to insert a draining tube because I developed a cyst. I was so angry because I thought, *I had the surgery, I lived, so why am I still going through this pain, cyst, vision impaired, can barely walk.* They then dropped the bomb: we think you should do radiation treatment. NO WAY, no—I refused. My family wasn't having it though, so I went forward with the plans. For twenty-five weeks, five days a week, at 10am I walked into the Mercy Hospital Radiation Therapy Office. I hated every second of it. It got way worse before it got better.

I remember completing those twenty-five weeks and ringing that bell like all the patients before me, after completing their treatments. My last treatment occurred in September 2011. I remember thinking about Job. At the height of Job's trials, his wife asked him why he was still honoring God after what he endured. She thought that he should've cursed God and died. I understood Job. Job's response to his wife was shall we accept good from God, and not trouble? Throughout my experience I honored God; I never blamed God for my experience. My cousin Andrea Jackson played such an important role in my mindset and healing. She visited me every day and reminded me of my life before cancer. She would play my favorite gospel music and tell me stories that would make me laugh. My inner circle would not let me die. They prayed for me when I was too weak to pray for myself. It was an experience that I never thought I would endure. It took years to recover fully and I am sincerely grateful for God's healing hands.

NEXT LEVEL: The next level came in the form of cancer. My relationship with Christ increased, my compassion for others increased, my faith increased, my discernment increased, and my wisdom increased. I was a new creation. I fell in love with God all over again. God healed my mindset, my body and my heart. I started seeing life through a new lens. I became vision-rich and execution-rich. It was a new day.

ATTITUDE OF GRATITUDE: Everything I lost was restored. I started doing keynote speaking again, my brokerage grew larger, and my income increased. I started traveling again and I actually completed my first book while going through treatment. I learned so much through that experience and I am forever grateful that mercy said NO!!!

I AM THE HEALED OF GOD!!! I learned a lot through this process and I tell my story everywhere I go. God is a forgiving, loving, merciful and gracious God. He can do anything but fail. I chose to believe his reports and not the reports of the world. I decided to take full responsibility for my actions therefore I made some adjustments to my diet and attitude toward life. To be Set Apart means God has singled you out. He isolated you from the others, so He can have some alone time with you and use you on a whole new level. To be chosen means He did the background check, therefore the views of others don't count. The only living God chose you. He sees more in you than you can see in yourself. Allow Him to do His job. I read a quote that stated, *God is writing your story; stop trying to take the pen from Him.* You see, being a single mom, living in lack, living with low self-esteem and self-doubt, being diagnosed with cancer—these are scenes in my story, not my whole story. God is still writing my story. I choose to move on, get past those scenes and not relive them over and over. This is what causes some depression: people get stuck in the same scenes and relive them over and over. My process was very painful at times, but it was my process that got me to where I am today. God restores. I am far beyond where I used to be, and I am grateful. Father God, thank you for setting me apart and choosing me. To God be ALL THE GLORY!!! AMEN!!!

Isaiah 54:17

No weapon that is formed against
thee shall prosper; and every
tongue that shall rise against thee
in judgment thou shalt condemn.
This is the heritage of the
servants of the LORD, and their
righteousness is of me,
saith the LORD.

Mary Murrill is a survivor, overcomer, and leader. In 1986, she was the victim of a gunshot that left her paralyzed. She divorced in 2012 and survived breast cancer in 2015. Despite facing such adversity, she never let the trials of life hold her hostage. In 2012, her tenacity prompted her to seek a degree in Business Management, which she obtained in June 2016. Her passion for liberating entrepreneurs and small business owners from the daily tasks of operating a business prompted her to start her own company. She is now the founder of Rescue Me Virtually, a company that collaboratively works with entrepreneurs and small businesses. Her services assist with organizing, maintaining, and marketing the business. Since the inception of her business, Mary has assisted an array of business owners in successfully building their brands. In 2018, she collaboratively wrote her first book, *A Threefold Cord Broken: What Happens When Christian Marriages Fail*. The book takes you on the journeys of seven courageous Christian women. Each gives a glimpse into their marriage, what went wrong, how they navigated the process as a Christian, how they overcame, the lessons learned, and where they are now.

Standing Tall from a Seated Position

By Mary Murrill

When I was 16 years old, I gave my life to Christ. I stayed in church all the time, not because my mother made me go, but because I wanted to. As I grew older, I still attended church but being a teen, I was into doing other things that did not align with the word of God. One day while working as a seamstress at London Fog, which was my dream job, I began talking to God. I was straddling the fence and wanted to get my life straight. I was contemplating, *What should I do?* On that Saturday afternoon, October 16, 1985, I made my decision.

It was a fall day in October, two of my cousins and I were spending the day together, and I was helping my youngest cousin with a sewing project. Sewing is something I always loved; my mother taught me when I was 9 or 10 years old. I enjoyed it so much, I enrolled at Mergenthaler Vocational High School and took a Needle Trade Course, which landed me my first real job, London Fog Clothing Factory in Clippers Mill.

Late afternoon on a Saturday, I was in the basement with my youngest cousin while she was trying on the garment she'd been making. My oldest cousin was upstairs. While talking with my youngest cousin I could see my oldest cousin backing down the basement steps. The fear I saw on her face is something I will never forget. I wasn't sure why she looked that way because I could not see past her. As I was approaching the steps, I could see her boyfriend waving a gun. He wanted her to go with him. There was exchange of words while we all headed up the basement steps, which led to the kitchen.

Once we were all in the kitchen, he stood at the kitchen sink with the gun in his hand, telling her to come with him. Everyone was in a heated exchange of words.

I picked up the phone on the wall in the kitchen to call 911, and he shot me, then my cousin (his girlfriend). She fell on me and then he ran down the steps and shot her sister, all while the 911 dispatcher was on the phone. When he shot me, it felt like my body lifted off the floor and I fell. I could feel the weight of my oldest cousin's body on top of me, and after he shot my youngest cousin, I could see him running out of the back door. The only thing I had running through my mind was my daughter, who was not there at the time. Unfortunately, my cousins' kids were there. I thanked God none of them were hurt. Once I fell on the floor the phone dropped out of my hand. As I was lying on the floor, I tried to retrieve the phone and the 911 dispatcher was still on the line. I told her I was shot, along with my cousins. She said the police were on the way. I was upset at the 911 dispatcher because I thought she was going to stay on the line until they arrived. So much for watching television.

Once the police arrived, they knocked on the door. I kept yelling for them to knock the door down, I could not get up. I was thinking it was because of the weight of my cousin on top of me, but it wasn't. Later I found out why. They finally came in through the back door, which was already unlocked, with their guns drawn. They wanted to know if he was still in the house.

I told them no, but they went through the house to make sure. Finally, the paramedic arrived. The first thing he asked was if I was sure I was shot. I told him yes. He said he couldn't find any bullet wounds. Finally, he found it under my left breast. All I could hear was I needed to get to the hospital, and they were trying to find where the nearest heliport was to land the helicopter. Still the only thing on my mind was that I had to stay awake for my daughter. As they were putting me in the helicopter, on my way to Shock Trauma at the University of Maryland Hospital, all I heard was, "Stay awake." I told him he did not have to worry about me falling asleep. I remember when the helicopter lifted off the ground and then arrived at the roof of the hospital, the doctors were outside waiting. They put an oxygen mask over my mouth and kept pumping. The next time I woke up I was going down a hallway with someone pumping the oxygen mask and me putting my hands over theirs trying to pump faster because I could not breathe. I had no idea that it was another day and I was going in for another surgery. The next time I opened my eyes I was on a striker frame being flipped over by a machine, and someone was putting a sponge in my mouth that tasted like watermelon, to keep it lubricated.

When I woke up again, I saw my mother, but I had tubes everywhere and could not speak. I had to write what I wanted to say. I asked her where my cousins were, but the writing was not legible. When my boyfriend came, I was able to ask him, but he told me I had to talk to my mom. I already knew, but didn't want to acknowledge, they were gone.

I thanked God for the peace I had during that time, but the pain of losing someone close to you is unbearable. Experiencing such a devastating loss had a part of me shutting down from getting to close to anyone, because of the fear of losing them some day. I do not want to ever have that feeling again. I know that is not realistic; however, that is how I felt at that time.

We were like sisters, always together. I was not able to attend the funeral since I was in the Critical Care Unit. I did not have the opportunity to say goodbye.

Once I was fully alert the doctors explained to me the significant damage the bullet had done. It struck my heart, lung, kidney, and stomach and landed in my spine. Although the bullet ricocheted through my body, I praised God that the only significant damage was to my spine, which paralyzed my lower extremities due to the swollen tissue that surrounded it. Even though I was paralyzed, I held on to what I was told by the team of Shock Trauma Doctors: that once the swelling went down, there was no reason I shouldn't be able to walk. I tried continuously to move my legs but couldn't; it felt like someone added a ton of bricks to them.

Even though I could not walk, I was grateful to God that I survived. Not being able to walk did not devastate me; it was the joy of being alive that consumed me. I thanked God for giving me an opportunity at life and to wholeheartedly serve Him without wavering. A new way of living was placed before me and I was excited to walk in it, with or without the use of my legs. After going through weeks of pain, heading to recovery, the only thing on my mind was, *Thank You, Lord!* When anyone came for a visit, I could see on their face they were not expecting me to be cheerful. I was the one cheering them up. Determination is what kept me from getting depressed. My focus was not on what I couldn't do; it was on what I could do.

While I was in the Critical Care Unit the nurses had to come and turn me periodically, so I would not get bed sores or develop any blood clots. For me to stay in position once they rolled me, they had to slide and stuff pillows under me. I had to learn how to roll left to right and right to left without assistance, which was very hard, but I was not going to be defeated. Waiting for the nurse to assist me could have taken all day. Being in pain and lying in the same position was motivation enough. Since I had to be in bed so long, I had to wear teds (white stockings that help with circulation). The doctors were amazed at how fast I was able to put them on by myself. It would take most people a long time to learn how to do it. Trying to lift my leg, which was dead weight, and stay balanced and put on those stockings at the same time was a challenge, but I did it!

Once I came from the Critical Care Unit, I was transferred to the Intensive Care Unit. While there, I had to learn how to sit up on my own. Every day I had to sit up for a certain number of hours. As the days went by, the time I had to sit increased. On this particular day, I had to sit up for four hours. I had not been feeling well and I explained to the nurses on day shift that I was having problems breathing. All during that day no one paid attention to my complaint. After four hours someone finally came to put me back in bed. When the night shift nurse, who I formed a bond with, had just started her shift, she came in to check on me and noticed something was wrong without me saying anything. She said, "Don't worry; everything will be all right." I thought, *Worry about what? I'm not worried.* I just had a problem breathing but it wasn't like I was gasping for breath. She rushed to get the doctor, and they took a blood gas. They found out I had a blood clot in my lung. If it had not been caught in time, I might not be here today. All I could do was thank and praise God for watching over me. The stay at Shock Trauma was for two months, until I was transferred to Good Samaritan Hospital for rehabilitation.

As I am sitting here writing this, I am thinking of the song, "When I think of the blessings of Jesus, all He has done for me, my soul cries Hallelujah, I thank God for saving me!"

When I arrived at Good Samaritan, I felt like I was at boot camp. I had to be up in the morning by a certain time, washed up and dressed. I had a rigorous schedule of rehab. Some days were fun, other days I hated.

The first thing I had to learn was to dress myself and prepare what I was going to wear the night before. Although I had grown accustomed to hospital gowns and teds, those white thick compression stockings, it was now time to start wearing regular clothes. When I first tried putting on my regular clothing it was uncomfortable due to the scar tissue. Having scar tissue with clothes pressing against it is very painful. For me to be comfortable I had to wear sweatpants and loose-fitting shirts, which became part of my daily wardrobe. Even though time consuming, it was much more comfortable to wear teds than putting on a pair of pants.

Besides struggling with putting on clothing, I also had to learn how to use the bathroom on my own—now that was a challenge. Since my sensation ended at my navel, I had no control over eliminating fluids or over my bowel function. I had to use a catheter to relieve my fluids and had a regimen for bowel care, while maintaining a sterile environment to reduce the risk of an infection.

After learning how to take care of myself daily, I now had to attend rehab to learn how to properly use my wheelchair. That was when I found out how to pop a wheelie, balance in place, roll while in midair, and why it was important. If I was ever alone and needed to get up on a curb that did not have a dip, I would need to pop a wheelie and stay in midair to maneuver my front casters over the curb before lowering on the pavement. It took me a couple of weeks to learn how to do this successfully. I also had to learn how to shop and use a Reacher to grab what I needed from a higher shelf without dropping anything and without assistance.

Once I learned to shop, now it was time to manage cooking without getting burned, especially since I had to be close to the stove and my reflex to move would be too slow. My mother made me an insulated pad to place on my lap as a precaution so in case I spilled something, I would not get burned.

After learning how to do all of that, I had one more thing I wanted to do, and that was to drive. I learned to drive, because although people were always willing to take me places, no matter a person's heart or intentions, life would happen and sometimes they would have to cancel, or I felt rushed to do what I had to do. I did not want to sit around and wait for someone to take me somewhere, so I took driver lessons to learn how to use hand controls, went to the motor vehicle department and passed the test. Next on the list was purchasing a car. God opened the door for me with Maryland Injured Victims Association, that made it possible for me to purchase a car and car topper (wheelchair lift) that made it possible for me to get around.

My stay in the hospital was a lot longer than I thought it would be. I was in University of Maryland Shock Trauma for two months: a couple of weeks in the Critical Care Unit and the remainder in the Intensive Care Unit until I was transferred to Good Samaritan Hospital in Baltimore, where I stayed for four months for rehab until I was released to come home.

Years have gone by and I have accomplished so much. One of my most memorable moments was when I found out I was pregnant with my son. Some thought I could not get pregnant being in a chair. Just because I could not feel did not mean that my reproductive system was unable to produce a child. My first pregnancy was prior to my incident and my daughter was born prematurely, weighing three pounds, eight ounces. Here I was pregnant again, and the circumstances were just about the same. I was afraid my baby would not make it full term because of my daughter coming early, and the doctor could not tell me why. To be on the safe side I acquired a doctor who specialized in high-risk pregnancies. I was blessed throughout the pregnancy and was able to carry my baby full term. At the time my water broke, I was unaware. I was home in bed not feeling well. I was in a little pain with a fever. I thought I was suffering from a bladder infection, which is common when you are consistently using a catheter. I called my girlfriend and she took me to the hospital. When I arrived, I was seen immediately; to my surprise I was told I was in labor. I was not mentally ready to have my baby. I still had a couple of weeks to go. My regular doctor was out of town, and the doctor that was filling in told me I would have to have a C-section. I told her absolutely not. She said I would need to push. I told her just because I couldn't feel below my navel didn't mean I couldn't push. She asked me to push, to make sure I could, before going to the operating room. After I showed her I could push she released the idea of me having a C-section. After three hours in the hospital, in very little pain, I birthed a seven pound, 11 ounce baby boy.

Having a healthy son, becoming a business owner of two businesses—previously A Tradition of Excellence Limousine Service and currently Rescue Me Virtually—receiving a degree in Business Administration, and becoming a wife, I can say I am truly blessed to have overcome so many obstacles. You can read more about my story in *A Threefold Cord Broken: What Happens When Christian Marriages Fail.*

I did not and will not allow my inability to walk to hinder me from doing whatever I want to do. I thank God every day for blessing me and allowing me to be a blessing to others. I will continue to Stand Tall, while in a seated position.

Jeremiah 29:11

For I know the plans I have for
you," declares the LORD,
"plans to prosper you and not
to harm you, plans to give you
hope and a future.

Kimberly Hobbs is an author, as well as a faith life coach, having a "heart's passion" to encourage and coach others to develop a more POWERFUL, connective relationship with their Creator. She has had interviews with Moody Bible Radio, "God at work" and various television appearances, sharing her stories, and she finds joy in helping others achieve their own relationship with God. She is the co-founder of Women World Leaders, a ministry which empowers Women to find their beautiful purpose God has designed them for.

Kimberly is married and lives in South Florida with her husband, where they own and operate their own Financial Coaching Business. Together they share a heart for missions, serving consistently in South Africa. They take teams of people with them each year to introduce them to "serving others" overseas.

Kimberly is an established artist, with much of her work reaching around the country and across the world. She helps raise support for her mission passion projects and her 138 orphan children she loves through Kerus Global. org in South Africa.

Kimberly and her husband have three grown children as well as grandchildren and extended family in the state of Ohio. For more information or to contact Kimberly, email: Kimberly@WomenWorldLeaders.com

A Beautiful Purpose

By Kimberly Hobbs

"Now unto him who is able to do exceedingly abundantly above all we can ask or imagine according to the power that's at work within us." Ephesians 3:20.

That POWER is the amazing power of God who works within each of our lives if we allow Him to. God's ways are not our ways and His thoughts are far better than our thoughts. Some of us may take a lifetime to learn these truths, and I am one of them. Through the raging storms of my life, God gave me a tremendous story. It wasn't until I began the journey of "writing out my story" that God brought complete hope and healing to me, along with restoration to my conflicted life and a deep sense of unconditional love from my Savior. Together, these breakthroughs showed me the extreme value which God placed on my life even before I was created.

Through writing, I have been able to learn that I am God's vessel, a masterpiece, set apart and chosen. I have a beautiful purpose in God's kingdom of life here on earth and on throughout eternity.

Prior to asking God for wisdom living, I lived numb on the inside, and this was a state of being for me for many years. To others who viewed my external life, my speech, my outward actions, everything about me to all who knew me, seemed to show that I loved God and loved my life. I basically desired a good and normal life and I convinced myself and others that I loved God above all else. Underneath, I possessed a penetrating, self-destructing fear that God didn't love me in return unless I was "good." My thoughts continuously spoke loudly and sealed that lie within me. *You're not good; your life will never be "good enough" to be a vessel, a certain someone "chosen" by God.* Understanding now those thoughts were lies, I can see God has a beautiful purpose for me, along with others. Back in my beginnings, how would I wrap my fingers around a purpose I never felt worthy of? One I wasn't sure even belonged to me? The fear of stinging disappointments that rose up against me, walking through chapters of my life, became hidden wounds I buried, many times over, without resolve. Those hurts fell into a place I locked up tightly inside me. Even though I would try to come closer to God, each time I made a mistake, I would beat myself up mentally and allow guilt to overtake me. The enemy capitalized on my mistakes and mentally used them against me, tearing me down with comparisons to other people and their lifestyles, and it wore me down emotionally. The lies from hell held me back and prevented me from having hopes and dreams and being a "someone" for Jesus, my ultimate purpose in life.

My dream in my late teens was to have a "Little house on the Prairie" lifestyle. I would have a husband, a family, live in the country, have lots of animals, love Jesus and live happily ever after. I quickly set out to achieve those goals and within a couple of years (my late teenage years) I married a man I loved very much. Innocence was our life back then and we walked closely with God. I gave birth to two beautiful girls while working hard at home and doing life in harmony with my husband. At a very young age we purchased our first home, kept busy in our church and lived a simplistic life with our growing girls. Eventually we were able to build our dream home, a custom log cabin in the country on five beautiful acres. We built a nice barn and had horses and lots of animals surrounding us inside and outside. My dream was coming true. I loved my new life, I was a stay-at-home mom, and I loved to take care of my home, my husband, and our children. I was "Suzie homemaker" to the outside world looking in. We all loved God and our family and simplicity was what we thrived on. No one outside our family came into our life. My life, even though simple, had all the beauty and elegance and appeal one could want. Our home life was wonderful, our church life was steady, we consistently read our Bibles and we taught our girls to love Jesus. Life couldn't get much better for me because I thought I had it all. People who knew me felt the same way. But this was only a chapter in my life.

It all fell apart when we took a break from God.

As active as we were in a very small church, we carried much of the serving load. We burned out. We removed ourselves from everything having to do with church and God, but only felt it would be a temporary withdrawal. The enemy had other plans. We thought we needed a rest period from church duties and commitments. We wanted to focus on our new home, some worldly friends we'd met and a new lifestyle out in the country. Church life became a drag and we slowly lost all connection to God. We allowed the enemies plan to take hold.

What had been our focus of life—God, family then friends—soon turned to absence of God in our home and our new way of living. We were having fun while living carefree from any accountability we once had while we were attending church. It soon became a very dark, ugly and painful time of living. The temptations we allowed into our home from "outside influences" became more and more challenging to overcome. We were haunted by our shame and without the presence of God in our lives, sin grew out of control, as we had no armor for battle. Playing with lustful desires and sexual entanglement within our marriage became more than our once-perfect marriage could endure.

The foothold the enemy had on my life grew into a monster of lies, deceit and wickedness. I couldn't give up the sexual addiction that had grown through this period of time, therefore our 20-year marriage crumbled, and I woke up inside another chapter in my life.

Through the challenges of losing my perfect life, I cried out to God constantly but felt He didn't hear my cries. My addiction to the sin that weighed me down was taking over my life. I even asked God to eliminate all desires for sex, so I would be free of this addiction. I just wanted my healthy, happy, stable life with my innocent family back intact but that did not happen. My life continued, void of happiness or joy. I'd go to church here and there, I'd pray sometimes, even often, but still felt "absence from God's presence."

One day, feeling like my prayers might have worked, I met a man who took my mind off all my worries. He was a charming, interesting and extremely wealthy man. He wanted to rescue me from all my sadness, to be my knight in shining armor. I went from being sheltered in a simple "Little House on the Prairie" lifestyle to a shattered, broken life filled with sin and shame to rejection and multiple wrong choices. It all led me into a life that would have a strong hold over me and a "sexual addiction" which dug its hooks into me so deeply that I needed something powerful to pry them out. The tool arrived and was a vast, unseen world to me, filled with new experiences and unending luxuries. It all lured my attention to power and money, so much that I could have never imagined it, not even in my wildest dreams. Some of the people I would soon meet and the places I would soon travel to were experienced only on television or in the movies and I was about to enter that door. Here opens another chapter of my life.

A relationship developed with this man and I moved in to another lifestyle. As time progressed, I found myself being fed quantities of earthly abundance. I soon became attached to the man who had shown me a completely new way to live. Although I never asked for a thing, I had everything a woman could possibly ever want as far as earthly pleasures. In what seemed like the blink of an eye, I was showered with brand new cars, Maseratis, Ferraris and Bentleys and even more than those. I drove them all; they were given to me. I barely would get used to driving one exotic car and another would arrive in the garage with a big bow on it, just for me. Whatever I mentioned I liked would show up with my name on it in one of the garages.

I was given jewels of all kinds, diamonds and more diamonds and a seven-carat engagement ring. Rolexes, Chopard, designer clothes of every style—at one time I owned over 100 designer handbags and collections of shoes like Louis Vuitton, Chanel, Prada, Louboutin and more. My closet was the size of a large master bedroom and it still couldn't contain it all.

I met movie stars, politicians galore and had breakfasts and dinners with some of our United States Presidents. I attended galas, political functions, Super Bowls and fundraisers, literally affairs across the nation.

I rode and owned magnificent show horses, even had some regular horses and owned several miniature horses. The minis I kept in an outdoor life-size doll house which I had painted pink. It was placed inside the enclosed tennis courts on the grounds where I resided. I didn't play tennis, but I loved occupying the courts with my horses. With such an extravagant love for all horses, no matter which ones I saw that caught my eye, they were purchased for me, each of them.

I lived in multiple homes in various locations with live-in housekeepers that took care of my every need. I slept on ironed sheets every night and never made a bed. I couldn't use a stove unless I practically begged to cook something I would crave from time to time from my past life. We dined at five-star restaurants, usually having at least two engagements for dinners in a day, with friends and acquaintances at every meal. We never dined alone, just the two of us. I traveled and sailed the world with people I met, and I sometimes felt I lived more inside planes than I did having my feet on the ground.

The more I was given, eventually the more I began to give away. Why not? I had more than I could ever want. I was given a biweekly paycheck (since I gave up my business to be with him), so I just gave the money away. I gave to church, to my girls, to family members, and I even gave to friends in need. It felt good. In hindsight, I tried to relieve the guilt of being absent from so many lives and present in someone else's. Although my loved ones were still around me at times, the emptiness inside me grew—an emptiness that was indescribable, having lived through it. I felt I was slowly losing my life. Comparing this life to what I had given up was brutal to me. I was haunted by my happy memories of the past and I was miserable! Though I once again appeared "happy and content" to everyone who knew me, I was dying a slow, disconnected death in reality.

The more I was given, the emptier I watched my life become. I compromised everything, and eventually lost my voice, the ability to speak up for what I wanted. I became silent in a world of opulence and festivities. My dreams and desires now belonged to someone else, their lifestyle, their friends, their religion. Of course, they all loved me and I loved them but I was still empty, void of my true identity.

Until...

Through a miracle, my life changed yet again. I was able to walk away from all of it: my fiancé of seven years, a lifestyle of luxury, furs, cars, money, famous people and more. How did I do this? This question is still being asked and it has now become my story, my testimony of how much God loves me. It's my miracle. I had grown to love a man who gave me the world but what did it profit me if I gained the whole world and lost my soul? That was the question I began to ask myself. I loved him, but I knew I loved God more. So what could I do about this?

My answer came during a trip to Israel I requested we take, my fiancé, along with my oldest daughter, my new son-in-law and a church group. We were in the garden tomb on the last night of that trip when God spoke to me in the silence.

"Do you love me?"

"Do you trust me?"

"Then walk away from this lifestyle and repent of it all. Your entire past needs to be confessed right now. I want your heart back, but I want all of it," God said. I heard His voice clearly. What seemed like an eternity sitting in silence in that garden was only several minutes long. I was trembling in fear because I knew what I heard and from Whom I heard it! I was faced with a choice.

Could I surrender everything to Jesus? Could I turn 100% from this life of luxury and being taken care of to a newness in Christ and dependence on Him? Could I let go and never look back? How would I do this?

Simply put, I surrendered all to Jesus. I just did it. I didn't know what or how, but I prayed asking Jesus to forgive me and give me the strength needed to walk into a life of serving Him without looking back. Right there in the garden tomb in Israel, I fully surrendered. My life changed forever, eternally. My burden was lifted, and the shame of my life was taken away. I was now on the road to abundant life and it was only the beginning.

It most definitely was not an easy road for me. I had to hurt someone very deeply by exiting a relationship where I was treated like a princess. Since we were not married and there were no signs of marriage coming anytime soon, I had to do what I knew to be right in God's eyes and move out.

Knowing in my mind I couldn't take anything with me, the fear began to escalate quickly. Where would I go? What about money? This man in my life paid for EVERYTHING but if I left, it all stopped.

With God's help I began to pray fervently, continuously, asking Him to direct my thoughts, my steps and get my life back on the proper pathway.

Focusing now on God and His Kingdom, I made the decision to serve Him with a purpose and a plan. I had to forgive myself and understand God did have a certain plan for my life and I began moving in obedience to what God was calling me to do. Jeremiah 29:11: "For I know the plans I have for you says the Lord, plans to prosper you and not to harm you; plans to give you hope and a future."

I did a complete halt in Israel and turned my life toward God. It wasn't me or anything I could physically do. It was God working inside me, the POWER of God. There is no explanation for what I had just walked away from and walked toward other than it took supernatural power to do so! I left everything behind. I took myself, my clothes and some things that were given to me and went and stayed at my mom's house for a few weeks. I knew God would take care of me, and He did.

God put the idea in me to write. I was not an author nor did I have any experience at that time, but I heard His voice through listening. He is what I heard. God was calling me to start over again with my life but now in South Florida rather than Ohio. I had to leave my current situation to be able to completely focus on what God was calling me to do. It had to be somewhere far away, without distraction. Within three weeks I found myself driving to South Florida and exiting the extravagant lifestyle I had known for seven years, I left extended family and 45 years of life in Ohio to soon find myself once again starting another chapter of my life.

Now I needed to detox from the residue of opulent abundance, and God led me to an old, grungy, dilapidated one-bedroom condo/apartment from the 1950s, on a quiet golf course community in Pompano, Florida. I was not thrilled. I put on my gloves and began to clean years of dirt and grime in that quiet place. With God's help, I was able to bring myself back to a "humble way of living" and it was there I allowed God to begin His work in me through writing.

Not knowing where to begin in my new writing journey, I prayed and asked God for a verse to launch my writings. I closed my eyes, opened the Bible and pointed down on the page to a singled-out verse. It was Ephesians 3:20 my finger pointed to on the page. I had never read that verse before. I had to ask God what it meant. I read it over and over for hours and hours. The same verse! Is this how I start my writing? I couldn't figure it out at first but God told me the answer was yes. It has now become my life verse and I use it in everything I do forward and it's my lead and my lean. "Now unto him who is able to do exceedingly abundantly above all we can ask or imagine; according to the power that is at work within us."

It didn't make sense to me but as I studied it, I realized what power God was talking about. It was the power I had from the Holy Spirit who now resides inside me. I began to write and write and write... through lonely days and nights, I would cry out to God to ease my lonely heart, and I wrote out my detailed story. My life began to heal. God gave me scriptures daily which I used throughout my book. Those scriptures, along with constant prayer, breathed life back into my soul. I secluded myself and wrote every day for hours upon hours for an entire year. True abundant living, though it took time, came alive to me. My life was finally changing and had meaning that I had dreamed and hoped for once upon a time. God was working through me. I began leading people to Jesus through my story and God got all the glory. I loved it. It felt right, and I felt loved. It was all about Jesus and giving all to Him. Everyone I spoke to, I shared my story with. True abundant living, though it took time, came alive to me and everyone who met me. Once again, people looked at the outward appearance but now they knew for sure who occupied my inward heart.

Although I loved what I was doing in writing a book, I desired companionship. I knew I needed to pray for a husband, a man I could do life with while serving God. I knew he was somewhere, breathing, walking around on this planet and that God was preparing him for me and me for him. He'd be the man who would love God more than he loved me. I trusted God; I believed Him when He said in His word, "If you ask for anything in my name, I will do it."

The man I'd receive would be a man who would serve God above all else, while protecting me completely and living a life of surrendered obedience. He'd be a man I could serve alongside while doing life together. He would be a man who would love me and understand my past and not be jealous of it in any way. A man who would love my grown girls like they were his own. A man who would desire to do missions with me, ministry with me and go wherever He felt God would call us. A man who would allow me to serve God in my own calling as well as together with him.

I prayed daily that God would bring this man into my life. Sometimes I prayed more than once in a day and often I cried to God for him in my loneliness. I even tried to help God but thankfully I realized quickly I needed to fully trust Him alone. God had me wait for years. I knew He had me waiting while He grew the woman that He wanted me to become. I wouldn't change any of that now. Surrendering my life back to God brought me the man of my prayers and the true love of my lifetime. Being set apart and chosen became a reality to me and the fact that I didn't have to do it alone was an answer to my prayers and a knowledge that God loves me deeply. Together we now travel the world. We help care for many orphaned children in Soshanguve, South Africa. We work closely with the staff of Kerus Global. We get to live in the sunshiny state of Florida. God blessed us with a huge home that we give back to Him for service with Christian family members who live close by in surrounding areas. We have started several ministry groups. The groups have grown and are touching countless lives. Joy pours into us daily, with people continually surrounding us. One group in particular led me to writing more over the past two years than I have ever before. I was able to write the book *Fuel for Life: Abundant Living through Daily Coaching.* My life's trials and victories through redemption have given me ways to become a great encourager to others.

We hold monthly tiki life groups outdoors on our property, poolside, which has now grown to maximum capacity, but we continue to fit them in with God's help. God continues to bless us with growth in our groups as we focus on Him. God has also planted a vision within me that has grown over the last year. God gave me a beautiful, dear friend who shared the same vision. It is a purposeful ministry for women and it is flourishing in South Florida and all the glory goes to God within this group. Women World Leaders has become a way that God is allowing me to "give back" for all that has been "forgiven" in my life. God doesn't require me to give back to Him out of demand, but I choose this because it's how strongly I desire to serve Him for all He has done for me.

I have the opportunity to encourage women of all ages, daily, to help them find their beautiful purpose in this lifetime. God has given me a gift of empowering leaders in the Ephesians 3:20 way: exceedingly and abundantly. I am able to do this because God tells me, "Now unto him who is able to do exceedingly abundantly above all we could ask or imagine; according to the POWER that is at work within us." I am overwhelmed and over-joyed each day I wake up to serve my King and Savior, Jesus Christ. I am forgiven. I am transformed into a new creation, one that I never could have imagined to be possible when I faced my darkest days. I am a nobody, but to God I am somebody. I am set apart and chosen by the One who loves me and values me the most. God has always wanted to use me. I had to travel this journey in life to realize it. God wants to use any of us who are willing to be set apart and chosen for His purpose. We each have a beautiful purpose to fulfill, one that God has planted deep inside of each of us. You are a masterpiece.

Ephesians 2:10: "For we are God's masterpiece. He has created us anew in Christ Jesus, so we can do the good things he planned for us long ago."

If God can use me, an ordinary woman, who started a simple life without any extreme goals, and now I'm doing extraordinary things, I can tell you truthfully, He can use you. You are an extraordinary person and if you seek out God with all your heart, you will do extraordinary things for Him. God says, "If you seek me, you will find me."

I'm grateful I found God while still possessing all my capabilities to serve Him in this lifetime. I know now that I'm set apart and chosen and I've realized through my journey it is for such a time as this.

··

Psalm 139:14

I praise you because I am fearfully

and wonderfully made;

your works are wonderful,

I know that full well.

··

Dr. Jiajoyce Conway is a wife, mother, grandmother, evangelist, author, teacher, preacher and Certified Christian Life Coach. She is the CEO and founder of Changed from the Inside Out Ministries, LLC, a women's empowerment life coaching ministry. Dr. Conway's life is devoted to empowering women and teaching them to embrace their place of purpose, greatness and destiny. She lives a life that is committed to education, empowerment and esteeming the lives of others, and that is an example of what true change looks like when a woman says "yes" to God. Through her books, teachings, and preaching she transforms the lives of women toward living their God-ordained lives and releasing their pain. Dr. Conway believes in the power of change toward purposeful living. She lives a life that demonstrates the power of exchanging pain for purpose, bitterness for beauty and fear for faith. Her life mantra is, "Purpose to Change and Change on Purpose."

The Ugly Duckling

By Dr. Jiajoyce Conway

The phrase "ugly duckling" is where I lived for so many years. I did not and could not see myself in any other light, and I definitely did not feel beautiful inside or outside. For years, since the age of nine, I carried around ugly scars that left me feeling bruised and damaged on the inside. *Damaged, ugly, unworthy and useless* goods—this is truly how I felt about myself as a young girl transitioning into womanhood. So much of who I was had been bottled up and contained, because at my core I felt like something was taken from me without my permission and violation had left me vulnerable, torn and some days feeling as if I wanted to rip my skin off. These feelings carried me from the age of nine well into my adulthood. On my own I did not know how to shake my "ugly duckling" complex. I did not know how to wash off the dirt and scum of betrayal, bitterness, and brokenness. For fifteen years I was stuck in the body of a woman who did not know how to truly love herself, forgive herself, and value who she was. The semantics of life became easy as I mastered how to smile through pain and take on the pain of others so that I never had to feel my own. I mastered the "ugly duckling" place of hiding behind the veil.

The open wounds of sexual abuse are real. They oozed all over every aspect of my being and drained the life out of me because life had been taken from me. My trust had been displaced and destroyed by human hands. For as far as I am today away from the trauma, it is still so very near. I can remember feeling the hairs on my arms stand up as I felt the premeditated thoughts of my offender staring at me, undressing me and tasting my flesh as if I was meat for his devouring. His presence repulsed me, but the power of his presence at my bedroom door was overwhelming. There was nowhere for me to go, and the feeling of being trapped in this space, and in his presence, was suffocating. His breathing was like that of a dog panting in the heat of a summer day, and dare I say that is how he smelled to me. Each and every time, every night, and more nights than I want to count or remember. His stench was nauseating and made my skin crawl. *God, please let me disappear, please just remove me from this misery. I am useless. I don't understand and even if I did, nothing matters. I don't matter.*

The dripping, constant deep pain of sexual abuse and rape is like a faucet that does not turn off, no matter how tight you push the handles of the faucet back. The pain pulsates in your ear like a heartbeat until you become numb. I was numb. I had to go numb in order to go forward and live. I had to become immune to the leaky faucet and just fit in where I could get in. There was no justice; there was no righteousness because the walls had to be silent of such nasty secrets and damage. *What happens in the house, stays in the house.* Dare I speak of such things, dare I speak of such filth and expect someone to believe me? So I learned to package my pain, fight back the tears, toughen my skin and dive head-first into a place of existing and not living. I had to process what that meant from the age of nine and well into my adulthood. Where I should have felt safe and secure in my home and with my family, I felt so shattered and displaced. I felt as if I was a visitor that no one saw or could even understand. I was a wreck to my core, with feelings of unworthiness, dirt, betrayal and disgust. I was not beautiful, awkward, skinny and not damaged goods. Confusion was an understatement to say the least. I did not even understand why I had to go through so much, so young and all alone. I did not understand why such an experience had to be mine to process and get over. I did not understand why I had to prepare myself for the day that I would have to share this with my future husband and children and have this make sense to them. This was a cross to bear that I did not sign up for. I don't recall getting the postcard that asked for my permission to have my life torn at the seams, my trust violated, my self-esteem devoured, and my self-love dismissed.

I worked for years to pretend that none of that mattered because my scars were not visible. I consumed myself in school-work and even allowed abuse to make me a vulnerable woman who needed the permission of everyone else to exist...to *be me*. There came a time in my life where it became commonplace for me to allow others to dump on me and treat me any kind of way, and even have me apologizing for their shortcomings. I needed to fit in and from family to friends, I compromised myself out of fear of what others might see if I let my guard down. Sexual abuse left me feeling a stranger to true intimacy and being comfortable with my sexuality. This angered me because I knew I was so much more, deserved so much more, and this was NOT it. I deserved to be whole and feel like a woman who was worth more than the sum of her life's experiences...painful experiences. It was not enough that he took something from me as a child, but I was allowing the thief in the night to rob my womanhood, motherhood and livelihood. I was empowering him every day that I could not forgive him or myself, and even more, I was keeping him alive. This was getting old, and not only did I deserve more, but my life deserved more. God deserved more from me. Not only was I letting myself down, but I was letting God down.

For nineteen years I did not face the pain of abuse and un-forgiveness. The "ugly duckling" had tucked her head down and buried the pain and shame, allowing everything else to cover it over like eschar. *Eschar is the dry, black, dead tissue that sheds or falls off from healthy skin after injury, typically burns.* In my own way I had been burned and now eschar had formed. For nineteen years I had convinced myself that this was a part of my fate that I was meant to endure, and what did not kill me, made me stronger. "We plan the way we want to live, but only GOD makes us able to live it." (Proverbs 16:9). Every day I managed to convince myself of this so that I could live with myself and the guilt of my shameful secret. However, there was so much more depending on me to heal. There were lives that needed me to be whole so that I could nurture them and help them to live their best life. My children needed a mother who had a true sense of identity, a heart that could love and receive love, and a mind that was sound and not tormented by the unpleasantries of life. My husband deserved a wife that was not looking for him to fix her or make the past better but loved him and appreciated him in his own right. I needed the facades to come down so that I could just be me. I needed to not just learn to love me, but to embrace who I was and whose I was as a daughter of God. "Before you do anything, put your trust totally in God and not in yourself. Then every plan you make will succeed." (Proverbs 16:3). My healing had to begin with me and God. I had no place or intention to forgive outside of what God would do in and through me. I was not strong enough on my own to see the best in forgiving and moving on. I was not strong enough to look past the bitterness and brokenness to be truly strengthened without God's help. No one can possibly understand how empty sexual violation leaves you if it is not an experience that they have endured. The loss of self that ensues at times can feel unbearable, unbreathable and an unrelenting pressure.

When everyone else in your life that you have given your best to shows you who they truly are, I am of the mindset to believe them. At my worst I thought I could trust in my family and believe that they would protect me. I trusted and believed that when all else had failed me they had my back and wanted the best for me. Interestingly enough, this has not appeared to be my truth from childhood and even now to some degree as an adult. All my life I have been there for others, and for the life of me, I don't know where those same people are now and where they were for me during one of the most difficult times of my life. I have been dismissed repeatedly, looked down upon and even scrutinized for my life's success, only to have found myself completely broken all over again in the same places of intrusion. So healing from abuse had to be intentional and even selfish. Healing for me had to be a commitment to self and to God that I would no longer accept what others wanted to hand me, impose upon me, or even attempt to make me own in the midst of their own misery. I had to make up in my heart, soul and spirit that I would let God have his way in my life so that I could live the best version of my life. "Remember the LORD your God. He is the one who gives you power to be successful, in order to fulfill the covenant he confirmed to your ancestors with an oath," (Deuteronomy 8:18). I was not living my best life as a prisoner to my own unworthy, unhealthy and unforgiving thoughts, but the shift was real, and it was about taking my life back. The "ugly-duckling" syndrome of abuse had consumed my life, as it was a complex about myself that had become a truth. Abuse was not something I had endured; it was becoming my identity. It was taking up way too much room on the inside and not leaving room for much else to form. The swan was waiting to unfold, and I wanted to meet her just as much as she needed to unfold.

"Fearfully and wonderfully made," Psalm 139, was God's personal conversation with me. Psalm 139 had to become personal for me so that I could truly heal. I had to begin to see myself as God saw me despite all that I had been through. The scales of my own self-defeating attitude needed a different view and perspective. I had become my own worst patient who had not mastered the concept of following my own instructions or those of God. I knew the prescription for living that I needed to fulfill, but I was fighting it kicking and screaming, to the point of exhaustion, only to find nothing was changing. So the antidote was finding who I was in the word of God. I needed to know how God saw me regardless of how shameful I felt about the secrets behind the walls. God knows all and sees all, therefore He was not oblivious to what I had been through and had been coping with for so long. Yet it felt new going before God and telling him as if He had no clue. I needed God to break me in my place of brokenness so that I could be made whole. Before pain stops, it peaks, and then there is an analgesic effect that takes place, then the place of pain goes numb and the pain ceases. I was tired of hurting. I was tired of the pain. I was tired of existing and not living as I smiled through the pain. My peak was here, and God's grace was more than sufficient for me to endure, survive and embrace my place of newness. I did not like where I was, and Lord only knows how I ended up here, but who else would I have wished this upon? It was my test and I was not waiting on God to proctor it; He was waiting for me to show up and pass. The "ugly duckling" was chosen and set apart, not for the abuse, not for the self-struggle and doubt but for the testimony of my life that has manifested—the testimony that would not only change my life but would leave a footprint in the lives of many women whose path I would one day cross.

"Vindicate me, O Lord, for I have walked in my integrity; I have relied on and trusted confidently in the Lord without wavering and I shall not slip." (Psalm 26:1). Restoration is a process and it is one that challenges every bone in your body and every breath that you take to heal, knowing that your life started out to fail and that there are people in your space that did not care if you made it. I still at times feel the darts and the unspoken in what people don't say, but can I tell you I live in an *I wish you would mentality* now. My healing, wholeness and complete happiness came at a cost and I *wish I would* care what others think or don't think about me now. I went through three phases to become the woman I am today: I got angry, I went through a phase of acceptance, and now I have an attitude of gratitude.

Anger made me face me and my un-forgiveness. It was my place of self-actualization and a reality check for me that I needed to stop giving power to pain and those who fostered it. Getting angry made me feel again in places where I had gone numb and died to my very own existence. Anger gave me the strength to move beyond the people, places and things that were not for me. The truth of the matter is that anger was the starting place of healing and wholeness for me, because it forced me to make up in my mind that I was better than what I was settling for. Anger forced me into the loving arms of God where I could surrender, submit and find solace.

Secondly, I embraced acceptance of what I had been allowed to go through to get to where I needed to be. *Acceptance* was not easy, but it was needed. Who wants to believe that they must go through hell and back before they can have true peace and happiness? I know I did not, but twenty years later I understand that God had to allow some things to manifest in my life because I don't know that I would have surrendered to God any other way. I would never have come to a place of being able to love myself as God loves me, sees me and values me. I spent so much time crying on the floor of a therapist and waiting for others to fix, validate and **accept** me like a fixer-upper. I spent so much time waiting for a *sorry* that was never going to come. If I did not accept me, nothing else mattered. Acceptance is not about agreeing with what happened, but it is about realizing that what you went through did not kill you or destroy you, no matter how bad the pain feels. It's about letting go of being the victim and embracing being the victor. I wanted my victory, I accepted my victory!

Lastly, I learned to be *grateful.* I am grateful for those who hurt me and those who have helped me. Those who hurt me made me grow up and realize my own strength. The pain that I have endured at the hands of those that I have loved showed me a greater version of myself. I was not this ugly duckling that I kept seeing through my very own eyes, but; to the contrary, I was a swan who in due time unfolded. I am grateful that in my unfolding I found the strength to hold my head up without shame, look others in the eyes during conversations and not feel as if they saw the vulnerability of my nakedness, and confess without apology that I am God's chosen daughter who is not the sum of her pain, but the totality of her purpose. I am not the byproduct of sexual abuse and violation. I am not the afterthought of someone else's mistakes and missed purpose, and I am not bent, broken or bruised anymore. I am grateful that God did not give up on me in spite of me, but instead He used my pain to usher me into my purpose. I cannot get back the years I spent existing in the shadows of shame, low self-esteem and lack of self-love, and not living my best life. Today I can be grateful for the time that I was set apart by God in order for him to process me, prepare me and usher me into His purpose-driven life for me. I am who I am today because pain did not win!

Psalm 27:3

Though an army besiege me,
my heart will not fear; though war
break out against me, even then
I will be confident.

Moana McAdams is a multi-passionate creator (*Burning Spear Boutique*), published photographer (*Overstreet Guide to Cosplay*), editor (*Wildcard Chronicles* comic series) and small business owner who advocates for diversity and positive authentic representation of indigenous peoples and cultures in comics and mainstream media. She holds a Bachelor of Business Administration in Management Information Systems with a minor in Computer Science, a Master of Science in Information Technology, and a Project Management Professional (PMP) certification. Moana is a bookworm who enjoys capturing life's precious memories through photography, traveling the world, and spending time with family.

Moana McAdams
www.moanamcadams.com
Instagram @thereallifemoana, @aftermathphoto, @
wildcardchronicles

Aftermath

By Moana McAdams

For Mom. Thank you for encouraging me to find my voice.

• • • • •

I come from a strong, independent, beautiful and fierce line of women. Generation after generation the warrior spirit lives on within each of us, waiting to be set free.

Kanaka maoli or *kanaka ʻoiwi* are the descendants of a powerful people who trace their deep ancestral roots back to the time when our ancestors navigated the vast ocean by canoe and conquered the rough seas before arriving at Nuʻumea, the remote chain of islands in the middle of the Pacific known as modern day Hawaiʻi. For hundreds of years, *kanaka* had no written language. The stories of our people and the history of our families were maintained through the beauty of oral chants, or *ʻoli*, passed from generation to generation. Hawaiians place the highest value and respect on our traditions, genealogy, and *aumakua* - family ancestor gods. With an acute sense of our connection to the land, Hawaiians respected the world around them and wrote many chants to celebrate the beauty of our island home.

I was born on the oldest island in an area called *Wailua Nui Hoano*, or Great Sacred Wailua, home to the high chiefs – or *ali'i* – of Kaua'i. It is a place of beauty and abundance that provided food and shelter for all who lived there. To this day, you can find the *heiau* or temples of our ancient *ali'i*. As in the past, *heiau* today provide a sacred space for the strengthening of mana and relationships. About a mile away, I grew up in the home my parents built on a cul-de-sac between the protective ridges of Mount *Wai'ale'ale* and *Nounou* Mountain, better known as Sleeping Giant.

Most people will know my home for movies filmed here like Jurassic Park, King Kong, Avatar, and more. But for me, my island was my family's kingdom, and, in that kingdom, I was the *hiapo*, or eldest child. In traditional times, the *hiapo* was given to their grandparents to listen, learn, and master the family genealogical chants, social and religious customs, *kapu*, and specialized skills of their ancestors. The *hiapo* would become a living history book, to memorize all the knowledge that the grandparents had to share. While other children played and learned skills, the *hiapo* studied and cared for the grandparents. Hiapo were taught to assume responsibility and would often advise the family during challenging times of illness and crisis.

Much of my youth was spent working with my father in my grandma's *lo'i kalo* — taro patch — in Kapaia Valley. I loved the outdoors and being close to nature. Caring for the land taught discipline, strength, and appreciation for the food you eat. Like many of the *kupuna* — elders - of her generation, *Tutu* spent much of her life working on the pineapple plantation while Papa worked in the sugarcane fields. They married and raised their family in "the valley." In addition to their taro business, they raised pigs which were sold off to other families for food to celebrate special occasions like birthdays or weddings.

On school days, my sister and I spent our afternoons with my grandma on my mother's side. She grew her own vegetables and harvested them fresh - farm to table in every sense of the word. Banana trees, carrots, beets, lettuce, and cabbage were popular foods on her table. *Konohiki* stream bordered her property and we often enjoyed fresh mushrooms that grew along the water's edge under the *hau* trees. We loved when it was time to help Mama rake the leaves in her yard because that meant we'd get to make a fire.

I was an adventurous and fearless little girl who often ended up playing with the boys more than the girls. The kids on my street formed a bike crew and we would race our bikes through the neighborhood like Cru Jones on the Helltrack course. I had an awesome blue BMX Mongoose bike and my sister chose a more feminine pink bike with the banana seat. We'd pretend the slope in our driveway was our ramp to do tricks and practice our stunts. When I wasn't riding my bike or working the land, I spent a lot of time at the beach with my family. Dad was a long-time fisherman, so the ocean was a second home. Our favorite playground was Lydgate beach, adjacent to *Wailua Kai*, the landing place where our ali'i of old launched their canoes and traveled back and forth from the island. Lydgate became a popular hangout spot for many families. A rock wall formation created two ponds — one was shallow enough to allow babies and toddlers the ability to swim safely. The big pond offered a larger pool to swim in, waves to ride your boogie board without getting swept away, and an amazing underwater colony of fish to be discovered for the skilled swimmer or snorkeler. It was every kid's dream.

In the early weeks of freshman year, my life drastically changed when our island was unexpectedly hit by Hurricane 'Iniki — a category 4/5 storm that destroyed over 1,000 homes and severely damaged nearly 5,000 more, leaving them uninhabitable. In the early hours of that morning, I remember sitting in the hallway of our home, huddled with my parents, my younger sister, and our dog. The howling sounds of the 140+ mph winds were intimate proof of just how powerful Mother Nature could be. Most residential structures in Hawaii were built with aluminum roofs and materials to welcome the usually gentle trade winds, so our island community was left extremely vulnerable to the strong, piercing winds of 'Iniki. The islands' steep mountains and narrow valleys funneled the winds and intensified their already brutal force.

I saw roofs flying across the neighborhood and wondered whether or not those families were safe or left vulnerable to the elements. Would we be next? I hugged my family for hours and hoped we had done enough preparation to keep us safe inside. The windows were boarded up as best we could, and the windows and glass doors were taped to minimize damage. The day dragged on as we sat listening to the deep howling sounds that seemed to never end. The eye of the storm passed right over the island, giving a false hope that the worst was over. The brief calm left you with an eerie feeling. We had minutes to survey the damage to our home and our neighbors before the winds picked up again for the second onslaught.

In the end, the storm cost an estimated $3.1 billion in damages across the state of Hawai'i and approximately eight thousand people were left homeless in its wake. The entire island went without power for weeks, many people for months. A month after the storm, only 20% of island residents were fortunate enough to have their power restored. I can still hear the loud humming chorus of generators throughout the neighborhoods. I remember standing in long lines with my dad as we waited our turn to get aid offered by the National Guard. For our entire island community, recovery was a very long process that took many years before full restoration.

Many families suffered huge losses in 'Iniki's aftermath. While our home withstood the storm with minor damage, my elderly grandparents lost everything when a huge tree fell on their home, leaving it uninhabitable. In less than 24 hours after the storm's departure, the number of people living in our small three-bedroom home nearly doubled in size when my grandparents and uncle came to live with us. Soon after, *Tutu* suffered a heart attack and was medically evacuated to O'ahu for critical emergency care that our local hospital couldn't provide. With no power and extremely limited resources after the hurricane, the situation was dire. Once admitted, her doctors discovered a foot injury that went unnoticed for days, due to diabetes. The whirlwind of events and short timeline led to a swift decision to amputate and prevent further tissue damage and infection. In less than a week, my family was saddled with new medical bills and an immediate need to make our home wheelchair-accessible for my now disabled grandmother.

In addition to the widespread residential damages, many businesses were destroyed, which led to high unemployment rates and limited resources for the community. My father lost his full-time job as a bellman at a four-star resort when new management took over and hired an entirely new staff. Suddenly, our family of seven was forced to live off one income in a state with one of the highest costs of living in the entire country. This placed a huge financial pressure on my mom to carry the weight while my dad searched for rare employment opportunities in a highly competitive, slow economy that was trying to rebuild after the storm. Dad's inability to financially provide for his family left him depressed and frustrated. It was such a huge burden to bear that there was no way to keep the stress away from the rest of the family. I spent most of my teenage life caring for my aging grandparents, working an after-school job to contribute to the family expenses, and trying to be a good example to my sister. Fun extracurricular activities were a luxury I could no longer afford.

My own dreams and aspirations took a back seat to bigger and more pressing family problems. My hopes to attend Kamehameha schools - a private school for native Hawaiian children - washed away when my mother told me I couldn't apply. As a child, I thought her reasons were selfish and that she didn't want me to leave the nest early. Looking back, I think she made the best decision she could, given the cards she was dealt. In truth, I played a huge role in our family's ability to survive such a difficult period. I earned my own money to pay for extra expenses that my parents couldn't afford, shuttled my grandparents to their medical appointments, and helped drive my sister back and forth to school and sports.

Despite the hardship and sacrifice, we learned what was really important - our lives, our families, our community, and the will to overcome and thrive once again. We were survivors, warriors who stood tall amidst widespread difficulty. I witnessed the courage and strength of my family and truly understood what it means to be 'ohana in the way of our Hawaiian ancestors. When someone needed a new house, the 'ohana came together to lend a hand. Our family loyalty and support kept the unit strong to evolve and respond to the challenges faced. Despite their inability to contribute financially, my retired grandparents built a garden and lo'i in our backyard to help put food on the table. We learned to live with less and remembered to appreciate the little things.

In Hawaii, only four out of five *kanaka* students finish high school and only two of those will earn a college degree.

Communities with a high concentration of *kanaka* are often the poorest regions in the island chain, with ~14% of the population holding a college degree. Despite this harsh reality, my family always encouraged me to pursue higher education. Before me, my mother was the only person of her generation to earn a bachelor's degree. I knew attending college would not be an easy task because my family did not have the money to pay for it. With my sister following closely on my heels, the expenses of putting a child through school were not going anywhere; they were only getting worse. At one point, my parents were forced into bankruptcy.

Taking the burden on my own shoulders, I applied for and won a few small scholarships offered by small businesses in our community, but it was simply not enough. Together, my mom and I filed the free application for student aid (FAFSA) only to be told that I was ineligible for true financial aid like grants since my parents "made too much money." That could not have been further from the truth. The only options left were unsubsidized student loans - the debt still facing many students today. With money being a huge obstacle, I had no time to waste. Every semester counted and while many of my friends could afford the luxury of partying, my head was always in the books into the wee hours of the morning. I balanced five and six classes per semester and carried a part-time job on campus to pay for my books, food, and laundry expenses. It was a heavy load but my upbringing and ability to overcome so many challenges gave me the resilience required to maintain my grades and complete the required coursework.

Although I pursued a technical degree, one of my favorite classes was 'Ōlelo Hawai'i — Hawaiian language — because we were not taught to speak our native tongue in our home. For my parents and grandparents, learning English was presented as the way for Hawaiians to "make it" in the modern world. Many *kanaka* were so convinced of the necessity of English that they punished children for speaking Hawaiian at school and teachers would even visit parents to tell them that they were holding their children back by speaking to them in Hawaiian. Learning my native tongue would give me the ability to speak with my *Tutu*, who was a fluent speaker, and it helped me to view the world in an entirely new way.

When I moved away from the islands after college to pursue my career, I was alone with no family around me. In the aftermath of my decision, the culture shock was disorienting and quite scary. In the DC area, there is minimal to no sense of community - at least nothing close to what I grew up knowing. People have a very singular "it's all about me" mentality. I missed the large family gatherings, listening to our *kupuna* share their stories that often left us laughing in stitches, the big welcoming smiles, easy access to the beach, and all the foods I loved. I was alone. No matter where I went, I walked amongst a sea of strangers. Most people would have given up and hightailed it back to the islands like the 14 other college students from Hawaii who chose not to accept their job offers. I was the only one left standing, with no mentors, no elders close by to guide my path. This was a huge turning point where I relied on my ability to adapt and overcome tough situations.

I began to look for fellow islanders in hopes of finding a tribe where I could feel at home. Eventually I found my way to a *hālau* - hula school - where I reconnected with my cultural roots and made long-lasting friendships that formed my extended *'ohana*. With this new family, I finally found a place where I could learn hula *kahiko* — the ancient style of hula that is not well known outside of the islands. Kahiko harnesses the *mana* — power and essence - of the person or place for which a chant is written and the dancer skillfully translates the story through the dance. This sparked a renewed and deeper interest in Hawaiian history and genealogy.

I started my own line of handmade island-inspired clothing as a way to feel close to the islands without physically being there. Each of my styles is named after a special person or place in Hawaiian history. Creating gave me the freedom to express myself, share the story of my ancestors in a way that evokes cultural pride and shared identity, and preserve our values to be passed to future generations. Through my business, I discovered a community of fellow islanders who grew up there or have a shared love for vibrant culture I am proud to be a part of. My customers are family spread across many different locations throughout the country, each of them an island, a beacon of aloha to remind us that the Hawaiians of old bravely sought out new lands to flourish and make a home.

After many years living away, I realized that growing up in Hawaii was a true blessing. By moving away, I rediscovered myself and found the courage to share my stories to leave my legacy that will hopefully continue to inspire youth for generations to come. My sister once asked me if I could do it all over again, what would I change? After giving it much thought, I told her I wouldn't change a thing. Sure, life would have been much easier if I didn't have to take on the level of responsibility that I did so early in life. Yet my experiences gave me the strength and perseverance needed for a career where I am almost always the lone minority woman in a male-dominated engineering field. Growing up in a diverse, multi-ethnic community gave me the empathy and understanding needed to advance in my career and lead large teams. Like my ancestors before me, I have traveled and set foot in many foreign lands where I connected with new cultures and discovered a global community of indigenous people full of rich stories that must be told. As my story continues to unfold, I honor the lessons of my past and look to the future with hope that my legacy will inspire the next generation and give them courage to battle their own storms.

Ku pākū ka pali o Nihoa i ka makani.
The cliff of Nihoa stands as a resistance against the wind.
Said of one who stands bravely in the face of misfortune.

Romans 15:13

May the God of hope fill you with
all joy and peace as you trust in
him, so that you may overflow
with hope by the power of the
Holy Spirit.

Yolanda Johnson is the owner of Beyond Measure, LLC, a consultancy that provides leadership, management, and diversity & inclusion training workshops.

Yolanda has over 25 years of experience in the vocational education, juvenile justice, and nonprofit sectors. She trains corporate legal professionals and oversees civic education programs that serve vulnerable populations nationwide.

Yolanda holds a Bachelor's degree from Bowie State University, and a Master's in Organizational Leadership from Nyack College.

She is a certified mediator, a member of the Society for Diversity and American Business Women's Association. Yolanda serves as Board President of Equipment Connections for Children, a nonprofit for disabled children. Her podcast, "Can You See Me: Women, Leadership, and Race" is designed to elevate voices of women from diverse backgrounds.

Yolanda grew up in Long Island, NY with southern roots in Georgia and Florida. She resides in Maryland and loves to cook, travel, and enjoy time with family.

He's Building My House
By Yolanda Johnson

"…. As we let our own light shine, we unconsciously give others permission to do the same." ~ Marianne Williamson

Many noteworthy things happened in 2007: Nancy Pelosi became the first female speaker of the house; Steve Jobs revealed the iPhone; and Senator Barack Obama announced his candidacy for the presidency of the United States, he would go on to become the first African-American President of the United States. All of these were turning points, significant moments in time, milestones in the development of future impact on the life of an individual, an industry, and a country. In 2007, I experienced my own set of turning points.

I heard Marianne Williamson's poem many times through Nelson Mandela's delivery. It was such a powerful message. However, I remember the day when I actually 'heard it' in 2007 and allowed it to interrupt my thoughts. I was sitting in a leadership development program. The facilitator had a habit of making us dig deeper through radical, engaging conversation, even when we did not want to. He knew that for us to be leaders in our jobs and in our lives, we had to discover places within us that sometimes made us uncomfortable. "Chris," the facilitator, was so full of humor yet so intensely intellectual that you could not be in his presence without tapping into a higher thought process of your own. So here Chris was on this day reading this poem and I heard him say "....it is our light not our darkness that most frightens us." Wait, what did he just say? As I looked up from daydreaming, doodling, thinking about my teenage children or in some deep thought about how I was going to make something happen, Chris was looking directly at me, or at least that's what it felt like.

Did you ever go to church and feel like the person delivering the message had been in your home? That's how I felt at that moment. Chris was in my life, in my business. He then went on to say, "... your playing small does not serve the world," and he's still looking at me. Ouch! Those words cut me so deep. ".... there is nothing enlightening about shrinking so that other people won't feel insecure around you...we were born to manifest the glory of God that is within us; it's not just in some of us, it's in all of us." Okay, that was enough. I felt a stillness in that moment that would not allow me to run, would not allow my thoughts to wander, and would not allow me to speak. Those words hit me with a fervent sense of consciousness that gave me no other choice except to acknowledge and absorb it. I knew that I had the ability to influence others. I had the capacity to change the direction of my life, my children's lives and those around me. I knew that I was unique, maybe even peculiar to some. But why had I kept myself inside a box, a box that held the gifts of my authentic self? Was it because of all the mistakes I'd made along the way? Did I not value myself enough or did I not believe that God's glory was inside of me? Was it because I thought I didn't deserve it or was it because I knew I deserved it, but I was so bound by the fear of what would happen if I opened that box to the world?

Ever since I was a little girl, I often shrank and watered myself down because I didn't want to show how smart I was (although I couldn't help it at times) or I didn't want to make a mistake or fail. I didn't want to show that I actually thought very highly of myself. I've always had a huge vision for my life, a vision that terrified me and still does in many ways. In that leadership class, at that moment, I realized that the fear was not related to external factors but to the fear of revealing my inner sense of greatness. I wanted to protect it and keep it hidden. I didn't want others to think I thought I was 'better than' anyone else. I chose not to pursue things I knew I was capable of doing, not because I didn't know that I could, but because I knew that I could, but I was terrified of what would happen if I did. I allowed life's circumstances to put me deeper and deeper into that box. It was my comfort zone, my safe haven, a place where I didn't have to show myself to the world; I didn't have to be responsible for the glory that God had given me.

I see God in many things: I try to see God in all people. I see God in plants. He speaks to me through water, through the beauty and tranquility in early mornings, and through others' pain. When I see other people suffering, it pierces my spirit and I believe that I actually feel their hurt. However, I am also able to see past the pain and suffering and see greatness in that same person. I keep these moments close to myself, wrapped up like a mother does a newborn child. I used to think that I protected these moments out of fear of being ridiculed. As I grow spiritually, I realize that my time with God is intimate and individualized for me; therefore, I am able to release myself from the expectation of trying to force others to understand it.

There is only one time in my life that I know I heard God speak directly to me in an audible voice. In 2007, during the same leadership development program mentioned earlier, we were required to attend a leadership training retreat on the eastern shore of Maryland. I was in the shower in my hotel room after finishing another day, an exhausting and impactful day, of leadership development training. Another provocative facilitator like Chris took us through an exercise where we had to imagine ourselves walking through a junkyard of garbage, old tires, discarded and thrown away items that no one wanted, when we'd suddenly discover a beautiful box. We had to use our own individual imagery to place whatever we wanted, something that we may have lost, inside that box. Initially, I could not think of anything that I wanted to see in that box; it was empty. I saw a mysteriously alluring box with beautiful jewels on the outside but could not see anything tangible inside. I began to think about being sexually molested, fondled by a man that was supposed to be a family friend. For many years, I would feel his touch; I would blame myself for not running out of the room, screaming for someone and for not telling my mother. How could I be worthy of all this greatness and leadership that everyone was speaking of? The greatness that I knew was inside of me, but I had not accepted? I wasn't worthy.

Yes, I had beaten some of society's odds despite being raised in a single-parent household and having no relationship with my father. I fulfilled my childhood dream to be a cosmetologist and a salon owner and became a first-generation college graduate while raising two kids. However, there was always a dichotomy running through my mind, a two-part story that gave me the ability to see the gifts of perseverance, resilience, and leadership with discernment that allowed me to see the gift in others. Then there was the other part of the story. The part of the story that I used to identify with the most. The story that told me I wasn't worthy because I 'allowed' a grown man to violate me at nine years old, I had two children out of wedlock, I had failed at business, and raising teenagers was becoming so overwhelming at times that I wanted to give up because I felt like I was failing at that too. God couldn't and shouldn't use me.

I placed my self-worth inside that beautiful box inside of the junk yard in that moment at the retreat. After listening to others speak about what they discovered or re-discovered inside that box, I got up and shared my story of molestation and losing my self-worth to my cohort. The facilitator ended the session. I imagine he understood that it was such a raw moment for me and for my colleagues. I felt like I was in a bubble with nothing but air. There was no fear, no hesitation, and for the first time, no shame. When the night ended and I went back to my room, I was still not totally conscious of what happened. I sat for a while to digest what I had just released to the group before taking a shower. I felt lighter, like I was floating, and my mind was free from ambiguity. As I was in the middle of showering, I heard a voice say, "I am going to build you a house." After a pause of only a few seconds that felt like an hour, I then heard, "But that house will not belong to you." The voice was clear, safe, soothing yet very unyielding. It reminded me of the feeling I get when I lie in the bed next to my mother, the feeling of peace and certainty, but this voice was intense, surreal and magnified. I am not quick to be certain of anything, but I am certain that God had spoken to me. But why me? Why then? And what did He mean by "build me a house?"

I am grateful for my mother, who taught my sisters and me about God at an early age. I did not always understand it or embrace it. We had Bible study in the home daily. If we were a part of after-school activities it did not matter; we still had Bible study. If we had company staying over, they knew that we were having Bible study and they would be a part of it. The funny thing is that they still wanted to stay over and, in some cases, they did not leave, perhaps because they knew that through the chaos of our home with six girls, my mother lovingly welcomed them, most often with a great meal. We went to church on

Sunday mornings, Sunday evenings, and Wednesday evenings while still having Bible study every night at home. I grew up in a church that gave me a good foundational understanding about who God is and what sin looks like. I heard a lot about repentance through Sunday mornings when people had to go "up front" and admit they had sinned. I heard stories about people being ostracized because they had bought shame on the church, on the body of Christ. Through my recollection, people in the church were not supposed to mingle with people who were living in sin until that person went "up front" and publicly repented. I don't remember a time where my mother shunned anyone. In fact, I saw her welcome people who ostracized her. I always wondered how the church could call someone a brother or sister and at the same time exclude them for their mistakes. I will forever be grateful for the foundation that was provided to me, but I knew that I had to find what God meant for me and to me. As I continued to journey through adulthood and motherhood, I began to study for myself. Although it was difficult to detach from the type of church that I was raised in, I found a church home that consistently taught forgiveness, restoration, and a path to God that was sometimes filled with things like self-doubt, feelings of unworthiness, guilt, and shame. Before I could understand what God was saying to me in the shower on the eastern shore in 2007, before I could forgive the man that violated me and erase the stain of his touch from my body, before I could forgive myself for my own transgressions, before I could accept the greatness that was inside me, I had to seek God for myself. My mother's relationship with God could only take me so far. Through bouts of counseling; developing my own relationship with God through study and prayer; learning how to speak things into existence; and learning that faith meant that I had to see past my current circumstances and believe that

God's plan, love, and grace for me is greater than any obstacle or mistake, I was able to understand that He was building me to influence others. My father died right after I completed that leadership training on the eastern shore. I lost the ability to connect with him, but I found peace. I found peace in knowing that my father was purposed to meet my mother by God to produce me. After we found out that my father died, my mother gave me a card that said that was her Job. I took time to study the story of Job in the Bible. I found that Job showed a lot of endurance through times of struggle and suffering, but he patiently waited for God and believed in God's love for him through the hardest times. This was all a part of God building my house. I found peace in knowing that God was still building me through every challenge and success, for me to impact others. God spoke to me when I was open to trust the process of life, trust that the pain was going to mean something. That does not mean that I did everything right from that point in my life; in fact, it means the exact opposite, but I held onto God's voice. Through every amateur decision that I made, through every disappointment, failure, and heartbreak I remember God's voice. I remember that being a leader doesn't mean that I will not fail, that I will not hurt or that everyone will see what I see.

Being a leader means that I will use whatever I have in me to positively influence others around me. It meant that I could not settle in the box of contentment. It meant that the moment of being touched inappropriately at an early age was not my story, being a young mother was not my handicap, but it was a part of building a house, a structure with a looking glass made up of restoration, resilience, and discernment. I believe the looking glass gives me a window to see leadership in others that they may not see in themselves. I knew that I loved to educate and help others to reach their own potential, but the fear of my own ability made me unconscious to the impact that I could make. When I release the fear of my light, I become conscious of how I can make a positive impact on the world around me. I do not have to have a large platform like Nancy Pelosi, Steve Jobs, nor did I become the President of the United States like Barack Obama. The platform that God gave me is equally important. A colleague once thanked me for believing in her when she did not believe in herself. Many people have told me this, but the most impactful part of what she said is that she was able to instill the same thing in others. She used what I gave her to help someone else. Because I was able to let my light shine, she was able to let hers shine for someone else. Her looking glass into herself and others became clearer through my light as it gave her a path of courage to shine her own. I have many accolades and accomplishments that I am proud of, but I have learned through my own walk that leadership is not always a pretty package. It is not about degrees or titles but about how you utilize what God has placed inside you to spread your light and help others.

Light bulbs and candles have something in common. The more light they give, the more they burn. This is what I think of when I think of leadership. Leaders must expose their own greatness to the elements. It is not free from self-doubt, criticism, ridicule, unrealistic expectations and sometimes even danger like that endured by world leaders like Dr. Martin Luther King Jr., to achieve a dream of an inclusive society or John F. Kennedy for his choice to speak out against segregation. Leadership comes in large and small ways. It is often visible, but it is sometimes quiet and hidden. It is often found in the most unpopular and unexpected places. God uses all kinds of people to fulfill His plans for others and to lead from wherever they are in life. God used my mother to show me what it meant to give to your community through opening her home and giving to others even when she did not have much. God uses me with all my blemishes and scars to lead people through management positions, community programs, volunteering, or simple daily connections. I believe that He is still building my house, building me to influence people in ways that I have not yet imagined. I will fight the fear and self-doubt that still creeps up within me to push through, lead by example, and fulfill the plans that He has for my life. I believe that I have the ability to influence my family for generations to come, through education, business, and wealth building. I believe that I can make a difference through community service. I believe that I can strengthen race relations by connecting and inspiring women of all races and socioeconomic backgrounds. I am thankful for knowing that fear will sometimes dim my light, but God has chosen me and set me apart despite my circumstances.

The fear of the unknown will never go away; we are human beings. There are things that we will inevitably endure when we expose our greatness to the elements of life. But the exposure, the light, will be a source of empowerment for those we encounter daily to expose their own greatness to someone else and thus change the world.

"What is to give light, must endure burning."
Victor Frankl

 **Desera Burney** is a native of Louisiana. She has 27 years of dedicated service in the Federal Government. She is a certified Project Manager and the Independent Business Owner of a Health and Wellness company.

Desera is an avid world traveler, a fearless and adventurous woman who enjoys participating in outdoor activities. She is a marathon runner and enjoys hiking, sightseeing and riding motorcycles. Desera is currently training to compete in a Body Building Bikini Competition.

She resides on the island of Oahu in Hawaii (Paradise). She is the lovely wife of 31 years to Thomas Burney, and they have three lovely children.

A Walking Miracle
By Desera Burney

The day that changed my life started at 5:30 a.m. on Saturday, June 14, 2014. My husband (aka King) and I suited up in our motorcycle attire and started our motorcycle journey from Maryland to Texas via a stop in Louisiana. We met up with my brother-in-law and the three of us headed south on I-495 for what I thought would be my longest ride on my own motorcycle (Red Diamond). We were going to ride approximately 1,700 miles during our entire trip. The weather was a little cool for me, so I had on all my cold weather gear. Oh, what a beautiful ride it was for us. After riding through Maryland, Virginia, and Tennessee we stopped for lunch. After lunch my brother-in-law headed back to Maryland and we continued our journey to Louisiana. For the next seven hours the two of us continued to enjoy the nice breezy ride, stopping for breaks as needed.

One particular stop stuck out to me and that was our last stop; as we suited up to get back on our bikes, an elderly guy told us, "You guys have some beautiful bikes; be careful and have a safe ride." We both said, "Thank you," and got back on our bikes and hit the road. About ten minutes after getting back on the interstate, my life-changing event happened. We were riding in the left lane on Interstate-65 and approached a yield lane that was merging onto the interstate; a car merged onto the interstate and got into the right lane and continued to come over into the left lane. They cleared my husband who was leading, but didn't clear me, therefore running me off the road. All I could do when I saw the car starting to merge on the interstate was say to myself, *Don't let them come all the way over.* The rest is a little unclear. I remember riding on the shoulder of the road trying to avoid running into the back of a car and then bracing to just let the bike go. The next thing I remember is sitting up in the median of the interstate with someone holding me up saying, "I'm a paramedic, sir; I need for you to lie down," and a lady in front of me saying, "I'm a nurse; you're going to be okay." The guy kept saying, "Sir, I need for you to lie down," and I kept telling him I was not lying down as I gasped to get my breath. I was having a very difficult time trying to breathe. The lady then read my name on my vest and said, "Oh, this is a female; her name is Queen Dee." They couldn't tell I was a female because my helmet stayed on during the accident. Both kept talking to me until the ambulance came, which was really quick. I know that God sent his angels immediately to protect me until the paramedics arrived, because I would have been there alone.

My husband finally made it back to me after chasing the car for a little while. He decided to stop chasing the car after looking back and seeing that I had lost control of my motorcycle and gone down. He parked his motorcycle and ran back to where I had gone down. The police arrived soon after and started questioning him and observing the scene. During his observation he advised my husband that I had hit not one, but two, cement blocks during the accident. The individual responsible for the accident has never been identified.

The ambulance arrived on the scene quickly, within 10 to 15 minutes. The paramedics immediately started treating me and asking if I was hurting anywhere. The only thing hurting at the time was my right ankle. All I kept saying was, "My ankle is hurting," and the paramedic said, "There is something wrong with your left knee; it is twisted." That would explain why I couldn't straighten my left leg. After being stabilized and placed on a spinal board, I was loaded in the ambulance and transported to UAB Trauma Center in Birmingham, Alabama.

Once I arrived at the hospital, the doctors immediately started treating me and running multiple tests to determine my injuries. I remember being asked a lot of questions, but I was in and out of consciousness. One thing I remember hearing one of the nurses say was, "I hate to cut her clothes, but we have to." I was wearing one of my motorcycle club shirts. They then said, "We're not going to cut her Harley Davidson socks; I know they were expensive." I thought, *Thank you.* Yes, they were and that was my first time wearing them. I then thought to myself that paramedic knew what she was talking about when she told me in the back of the ambulance, "Let's try to take your nice Harley jacket off, because they will cut it off you once you arrive at the hospital."

After going through an array of tests for hours, I asked the nurse if my husband had made it to the hospital. She replied, "Yes, he's here and we've provided him with updates." I then asked if I could see him. She replied, "We have a few more tests to run." I asked her if she could tell him I was okay. I knew he was worried about me, because he had to stay at the scene of the accident to finish answering questions and take care of my motorcycle that had to be towed away.

I was able to see my husband after hours of being examined. Both of us were relieved to see each other even though I was on medication, going in and out of it at the time. The next seven days were life-changing for both of us. The test results were still being received until the following morning. My initial reported injuries were a left tibial plateau fracture, right ankle fracture, fractured ribs and a punctured lung. I was advised that I would have surgery the next morning on my left tibial plateau. When the doctor came to discuss my surgery, he stated, "Your collarbone is also broken in two spots and will require surgery as well." He explained to me that both surgeries were going to require me to have plates and screws put in to stabilize the broken bones during the recovery. That immediately freaked me out, so I asked, "When will the plates and screws be removed from my body?" He replied, "They will be permanent." I replied, "Permanent?" and then asked, "Do I have to have the surgery?" The thought of plates and screws remaining in me was overwhelming. Within a couple of hours, I was off to have both surgeries done at once and with God's grace, both went well. The next day a team of doctors stopped in during their morning rounds and advised us that I also had an injured spleen. Therefore, a tube was inserted on my right side through the rib cage for drainage. I was closely monitored for the rest of my stay in the hospital, ensuring a few other complications didn't worsen.

The day finally came for the doctors to discuss my discharge treatment plan with us. During the discussion we were advised that I wouldn't be able to immediately travel back to Maryland. Therefore, they recommended that I spend the next two weeks in rehab unless we had other lodging options until I cleared several post-op appointments. Since I had an uncle and aunt living in the area, we were blessed to be able to stay with them for the two weeks. They also advised that someone would be required to give me the blood thinner injections in my stomach twice a day. I immediately told them I couldn't give myself the shots. Well, my King stepped up to the plate and learned how to give me the shots. I can't thank God enough for providing me with a husband who was committed to doing whatever was needed to take care of me during that traumatic time.

My road to recovery was very challenging and interesting. The next six months was a testimony. After spending two weeks at my uncle and aunt's home in Alabama, I was released to a doctor in Maryland. Thank God for the accident being close to family, because I don't know where I would have gone when I got released from the hospital for those two weeks. I am also very thankful for some true friends that spent their Fourth of July holiday weekend to come pick us up in their RV, since my travel options were limited because of my injuries.

Prior to going home, we arranged to have a hospital bed delivered. The doctors predicted that I would be bedridden for the next 12 weeks before starting to walk again. For the next four months our living room became me and my husband's bedroom. He refused to sleep upstairs in our bedroom; therefore, he slept on an air mattress right beside my bed until I was able to go upstairs.

During this long and intense recovery stage, my King became my sole provider. When I say sole provider, that's exactly what I mean. I had to totally depend on him for everything due to my injuries confining me to the bed. Out of the four extremities we have I was only able to use one, which was my right arm. I couldn't lift anything with my left arm due to the shoulder injury and couldn't put any weight on either leg due to the knee and ankle injury. My injuries were overwhelming to me.

I recall being told at the hospital that I would have to learn how to walk again after not walking for 12 weeks. That statement was hard for me to process, not really knowing what to expect. So when the day finally came, and the home health nurse arrived at our house, I was a little nervous. I asked God to give me the strength needed to do whatever was required of me that day. When the nurse asked me if I was ready to get up and walk, I replied, "Yes," even though I was still nervous. My husband proceeded to help me get out of the bed to my feet. I was then told to get my balance first before trying to take a few steps. This feeling was so weird. My legs were weak and felt and looked like Jell-O. With my King holding me up I took a few steps and immediately returned to the bed. I literally had to process in my mind how to move my feet to walk. The things we take for granted weren't so automatic for me at that moment. All I could say was, "Thank You Jesus." The next day I started using the walker, with a very slow stroll, which got better as the days passed.

> *The one question I was consistently asked during my hospital stay by doctors and nurses was, "Do you work out?" When I replied, "Yes," they would always say, "We can tell and that's a good thing. Otherwise, your injuries would be worse." I immediately made a mental note that I would work out for the rest of my life if I was able.*

The next phase of my journey became another thankful moment for me; I no longer had to receive the blood thinner injections in my stomach twice a day, "Thank You, Jesus". I was referred to Physical Therapy for rehabilitation of my tibial plateau and ankle injuries. During my initial visit with the therapist she examined me and reviewed my medical records to determine what treatment plan was needed for my recovery. She was astonished how far I had already progressed. She advised me that the ankle fracture I had was one of the worse, because of the location. My initial treatment plan was pool therapy, consisting of non-weight bearing exercises, since I still couldn't put all my weight on either leg. Another moment of taking things for granted. I had to be pushed in my wheelchair to the pool and then needed assistance with getting into a chair that would be lowered into the pool to begin therapy. This was another very anxious moment for me. I didn't know if I was going to be able to stand up alone, because I had only been standing with the assistance of the walker.

I continued therapy for approximately four months, going through several stages of progression. The struggle and pain I endured during the progressions was real. I remember being told to do the simplest things and wasn't able to do them. That was so frustrating to me, but I was determined not to let it get the best of me and pushed through until I either finished them or until the therapist felt it was enough. The therapist kept reassuring me that it was okay if I couldn't complete them all right away and that I would eventually be able to complete them with ease.

While keeping the faith and believing, I knew I was going to overcome all my challenges and my injuries would be healed. For about two months my husband had to push me in my wheelchair to my therapy appointments. One day he pushed me to my appointment and I was feeling pretty good, so when the therapist came to start my session, I asked her, "So when do you think I will be able to run again?" She looked so shocked and said, "Run? We need to concentrate on getting you back to walking. You have some major injuries that must heal."

As I continued therapy and my injuries improved, I became able to walk to my appointments with a cane. No more wheelchair for me! I was super excited now and looking forward to my next improvement. My therapist arrived, examined me and started explaining my next month's treatment plan. I asked, "Do you think I'll be able to wear heels by May?" She looked shocked again and said, "Why May?" I said, "My daughter is getting married and I need to be able to wear heels." She responded, "Your injuries were serious, ma'am, and they will take a long time to completely heal. You have a long road ahead of you. Let's plan on walking down the aisle without your cane, not in heels." So I finally realized that it really was going to take a while before all my injuries were completely healed. During one of my sessions in December the therapist advised me that I was being released from physical therapy, because I had worked hard and completed all necessary treatment plans. There was no further assistance she could provide to me. Although I was not at 100 percent, I thanked God daily for blessing me in my recovery thus far!

I was then released back to work part-time after being off for six months. I was ecstatic to hear the news, but a little saddened because I knew I still had a long road ahead before my recovery would be complete. I was still walking with my cane, so I took it easy for the next few months, as I got back into my normal routine. The next five months I continued the healing process with at-home exercises.

I eventually started back training for a 5K run. Prior to my accident I had been training to run my first official 5K in September 2014, but due to the accident I wasn't able to participate. After the accident I was determined to still run an official 5K one day. After training very hard, the day finally came; on Saturday, September 26, 2015, I accomplished my goal by completing my first official 5K. It was a very challenging race with lots of hills. I had run several 5K races, but this had been the toughest one of them all. *My participation in the race was delayed but not denied!*

After being introduced to Total Life Changes, an all-natural Health and Wellness company, I decided to join the company and became an entrepreneur. Joining this company inspired me to start living a healthier lifestyle. I started making healthier food choices and consistently exercising while continuing to recover from my injuries. During my journey of transitioning to living a healthier lifestyle, I relocated to Paradise, "Hawaii".

Shortly after arriving on the island I decided to take my lifestyle to another level. I incorporated using my TLC products along with my new lifestyle and lost 20 pounds. At that point, I would say that my injuries were almost completely healed, although there are still things that I'm not able to do without having pain or flare-ups of swelling. After working out consistently for 10 months, I started training to compete in a bodybuilding bikini competition. I developed an interest for the sport about a year ago. The competition that I was prepping for was scheduled for April 2018. After being faced with a torn bicep tendon and a partial bicep tear, I had to stop training and couldn't compete. I am currently prepping to compete in the same competition in April 2019. *The first competition was delayed, but not denied.*

Throughout this tragic event in my life I have NEVER asked, "God, why me?" It has humbled me and given me a whole new outlook on life. He spared my life and kept me here for a purpose. Therefore, I just want to encourage and motivate people to live a healthy lifestyle and believe that DENIALS are just DELAYS. All dreams are possible!

 **Danielle Batiste** is a bestselling author and speaker. She is a native of Louisiana, currently living in Newport News, Virginia, with her husband Floyd and son Brandon. Her husband and son are very much a part of her "why." In fact, they are her inspiration to serve the world as a speaker and author.

Like many veterans, of the United States military, Danielle and her family have been exposed to the pitfalls of being committed to both family and country. Deployment is a tough experience for the entire family, including the soldier, and not many outside of the military life fully understand the effect on a family member, not only being absent but being in dangerous, possibly deadly locations.

It is from these experiences that Danielle, known as Chardonnay to literary audiences, has written her bestselling and highly acclaimed books, *Cryin' Out-Separation Anxiety*, *The Soldier's Child* and *Let Go My Glucose*. These books give a candid real-life experience into her life and family.

No Longer Behind the Scenes

By Danielle Batiste

I have been a shy girl all my life. I think most of it came from being the oldest child and my mom and grandmother sheltering me from so many things. I was a shy person who moved away from crowds and preferred to be alone. I liked my own company just fine. I just did okay in school, but I was not a failing student either. I did not like math or English. You could see me sliding in my seat afraid that I would be called to answer a question and feeling terrible if the answer I gave was wrong. My body would tense so badly I thought I was dying. I later found out I was a bucket case and had bad panic attacks when it came to doing things that would put me in the forefront. English was not my best subject, but I passed, and I survived high school, shy and all.

My grandmother told me to find a job after I graduated, can you believe I signed up to join the military? I figured this would help me with becoming Danielle and not withdrawing into myself. I was that person that would come home from school or even on weekends and just sit in the house with my grandmother and do nothing and be very content. I didn't care to have conversation with the outside world, besides my family, and I don't know why I felt like that, but I was happy. When attention was focused on me, I didn't know how to handle it so I would just curl up into myself and say nothing and try to revert it back off me. I did everything in the military from start to finish, made great friends, lived a good life, travelled all over and I still felt like I couldn't get out and express myself because of my shyness.

Sometimes I also felt like I wasn't put in any position to come out of my shell, and I was happy with that. Nevertheless, I stayed in the military for seven years and continued to live my life on the sidelines. Now don't get me wrong, I had a lot of fun in the military and I also learned about business and bought my first condo at the age of 24. It's amazing to me how business just came naturally to me. I put all my time into it and I learned it almost all on my own. One person who I called my sister helped me as well. I even took a Real Estate course, but I thought to myself, *You do not like to talk to people so how are you going to be in a field where you must come out of your shell and talk to people?* I took the course but never did anything with it because I talked myself out of doing it, not wanting to deal with people. I know in many forms of life you're going to have to deal with people and can't shy away from it but when you have a deep fear of being in the forefront, or giving a school speech on your report, it was downright scary for someone like me.

After my time in the military, some of the shyness disappeared, but not all. I'm not going to say I didn't go around people period, but I was a very, as some called it, anti-social person and liked to be in my own company; that way I was not involved in any type of conversation. I went on to have many jobs. All were behind the scenes jobs, nothing too fancy, but what I did I got recognition for, so I knew I had the potential to do more and realized I needed to come out of my shell and get to work.

The transformation into the new me began. The first thing I did, which was something I never thought I would do, was write my first book, *Cryin' Out*. This from someone who did not like English in school. As a matter of fact, I did not like any subject in school. With writing that book, there was still some of the shyness that kept me from promoting and marketing it. My manager had set up a few interviews for me. I was shaky and scared to do the radio shows. Some were done by telephone—how can you be nervous with that? I was more nervous about what I would sound like. Would my words come out right? Would what I was trying to convey be received well? All of that can add pressure to an introvert. I had a few magazine interviews; still, everything was the same for me. I kept hearing, "If you do it enough things will get better," but in my head, I was looking for perfection. I was making things hard for myself.

I remember doing a book signing and a meet-and-greet. We had to get on stage and tell a little bit about ourselves and our book. Well, I was shaking and nervous and it was all in my voice, and I tried to do what I was told about looking at one person and talking to that person like you are having a conversation and it will make it easier. For me, the fright was so strong that it did not work. They were just people; what could they do but listen to my story? I made it through, but I vowed that I needed to do better with my public speaking. I was glad I went through that because it showed me I still had some hang-ups with myself. The more my manager pushed me to do things, the more it seemed I'd clam up into myself. I would try to psych myself up to do the different things that were asked of me, but you can rest assured, I did it with sweaty hands and was not sure of myself. So I had a long talk with myself about why I wrote the book and that there was a need for it and I needed to get out there and let the world know about me and this book because I did not write it for myself to read.

The journey for me began in trying to market both of my books. I began working on turning the first book into a movie. It has been a three-year journey with *Cryin' Out,* but I think the time will finally come. I still thought about how I was going to be in the public eye, talking about this book, when I like to be behind the scenes, and this was going to be a new way for me to be in the spotlight and carry this book, with everything in me, to get it to reach the top. How could a shy person do that? Well, I was going to have to swallow all my shyness and be in front of a camera and tell my story of how the journey from book to film happened.

I had to find the words and practice a lot of times in front of the mirror, but what I found with that is that practicing in front of the mirror and being in front of people are two different things, and what you say in the mirror is totally different from what comes out in public. Now that both books were out, I had no choice but to come out to the world and let them know who I was and share my story.

Telling my story was scary at first but it took the second book for me to come out and evolve into someone I did not even know I was. I began talking and talking and the new Danielle emerged. All I could think about was how this small-town girl, who never thought she would be writing anything, now had two books, with one soon being made into a feature film.

This dream was way out of reach and never a thought. I feel like a flower that only had a seed in the beginning but with time, love, attention and never giving up, I was watered and have blossomed into a full-fledged flower that can handle her own.

. . . .

James 1:2-4

Consider it pure joy, my brothers

and sisters, whenever you face

trials of many kinds, because you

know that the testing of your faith

produces perseverance.

Let perseverance finish its work

so that you may be mature and

complete, not lacking anything.

. . . .

Master Coach, Blogger, Author, Speaker, Trainer and #CEOMomma **Tamara C. Gooch** is the Founder and CEO of Pink Pearl, LLC, a transformational movement that magnifies the triumphant voices and stories of women with boldness, confidence and truth. With PheMOMenon At Forty blog & The Savvy Entrepreneurs Incubator group, a think-tank, next-level innovative learning platform, Tamara has established the concept of online community building and engagement, building and creating an elite, high-result society of everyday women who are impacting the world in monumental ways. Her formula for success is simple – Faith, Fierceness, Fearlessness, Fabulousness, Action and incessant Education. Tamara propels her clients forward with the blueprint and tools needed to launch and grow a successful business and monetize their genius in the most efficient way, while enjoying their lives, time with family, and a lifestyle of freedom.

The Woman Behind the Smile

By Tamara C. Gooch

No young lady ever wakes up thinking of or focusing on all the challenges and struggles she might face as a woman. At that tender age, we live our lives carefree, no heavy struggles or trials other than what to wear or what makeup to choose. We live our lives as ordinary, everyday women. Grow up, get educated, get married, have a family, enjoy your career and live life, right?

Our lives and the many things we experience have a way of shaping who we become. They shape our character, our emotions, and our responses, and if we aren't careful, we begin to hide behind the mask. We hide behind a smile and the response most women use when asked the question, "How are you?" "Blessed and highly favored!"

You see many of us have mastered the art of smiling our way through our challenges. We attend church, recite scripture, sing praise and worship, smile, speak and hug everyone we see, then leave church still doubting.

You may be asking "Why would she say this?" "How does she know this happens?" or "What woman really does that?" Well, the reason is because I lived it; it was me. I was that woman who hid behind many different masks, with the beautiful smile. Yet no one knew the internal struggle and fight between flesh and spirit that took place weekly.

How many women can you think of at this moment who are dealing with some trial, some hurt, some challenge in their lives, right now? Or maybe that woman is you?

You see we can come from the best of backgrounds and still grow up making the wrong decisions that place us in situations where the only thing we can do is cry out to God or someone for help. I was that girl, that woman, that mom, that wife who others looked at as a strong person. And growing up in an African American household you were taught to be strong, to withstand the storms of life. You go cry it out in the bathroom, clean your face, and come out ready to tackle the world.

I was that young woman who allowed those challenges to linger still within. I knew or felt that somehow, I needed to deal with those internal things but would go back to what I was taught. So, I suppressed it and smiled, went to work, did what I was supposed to do, pleased those around me. Yet, I went home and cried almost every night, miserable, stressed, unhappy. It happened so much it became part of my life's story and a part of my daily routine. However, I was in church, praising and getting my worship on while crying and others thinking I was so filled with the spirit and being moved by the spirit.

You see the challenges I faced I later realized stemmed from my teenage years and wanting to be accepted, wanting to people please. Well that part of me spilled over to my adult life without me even knowing or recognizing that was something I was doing. Because this story of challenges, hurt, pains, turmoil could possibly go into an entire book I will spare you and give you a time line of it all.

Age 15 ~ I lost my virginity, tried my first drink, and marijuana

Age 17 ~ I dropped out of high school

Age 18 ~ I met who I thought was the love of my life, and noticed the first signs of abuse and started doing drugs and drinking more in order to escape

Age 19 ~ I got pregnant, still red flag signs of abuse

Age 20 ~ I had my first child

Age 22 ~ I went back to school to get my high school diploma

Age 26 ~ I got married to my daughter's father (still experiencing verbal, emotional & psychological abuse, yet never wanted to be a statistic or a single mom)

Age 27 ~ I got separated after 10 months of marriage and briefly dated a guy whose father sexually assaulted me

Age 27 ~ I tried to make it work with my husband. Four months later I got a divorce, after all the years of ignoring the abuse, until my health started to be affected by it.

Ages 27 – 32 ~ I was single and decided to enroll in college. Still dealing with past abuse, now adding to that being a single mother. My continued coping mechanism was drugs and drinking while studying and parenting.

Age 32 ~ I tried online dating and met someone promising seven months in.

Age 33 ~ I got married to who I thought was my online knight in shining armor, the man who I thought God had sent me. I experienced the worst abuse and assault, rape, control, isolation, terror and came as close to murder as you could ever imagine.

Age 33 ~ (three months later) I escaped abuse and moved back to Michigan from Florida with my daughter and niece. I was homeless, jobless, without a car, and had only $396 in the bank. I contemplated suicide.

Age 34 ~ The reality hit that I was a single mother all over again, homeless, with no money, no job, and no family members, other than my parents, who opened their home to let me and my girls live there until I got on my feet. I slept in my parents' basement on a chaise lounge, my daughter slept on a blow-up mattress and my niece slept on the couch.

Age 34 – 38 ~ I tried to rediscover myself and heal from the years of abuse, people pleasing, being ostracized, rejected, the sexual assault and the internal damage that sat there for years. During those years I joined a new church where I decided to focus solely on following Jesus, serving and seeking Him in a way I had never done before. I was asked to work on different committees to work alongside someone who I formed a bond with and we became best friends.

Going through so much pain and hurt, one would never think their story would help someone else to overcome. How God could use them to impact so many other lives? Yet again God showed himself to be faithful in all His ways. The question was, was I ready for what God had planned for me? The answer was a huge NO!

While attending my new church I knew I needed to surround myself with other wise women of God. My mother suggested we start attending women's Bible study. It all started out so wonderful, great lessons, but when the time came, and I was asked to pray, I didn't feel worthy of praying. The internal damage was so deep I didn't feel like God would hear from a woman like me. But I kept attending Bible study, kept praying, kept doubting, kept worrying about my life, my future, and kept crying. Obviously, crying became a running theme in my life, my way of release, but as soon as I was done releasing it, I picked it all back up. Pointless, right?

That very year of feeling unworthy of praying, God used one of the women in Bible study to ask me to come and speak with the women at the facility where she worked. Again, I thought I wasn't qualified to do such a thing, considering all that I had gone through. I still did not understand who I was in Christ and how God was using my past as a platform for my future blessings. The decision took me three months to make, as I shared with her that I didn't feel my story was worthy of my standing on anyone's stage and speaking to other women. I didn't feel worthy of sharing my testimony with anyone. I looked at it as embarrassing, shameful, that all my business would be out in the open.

I didn't know or understand how God uses others to show himself in a way that truly blows our minds. Remember, He operates with the end in mind and redirects us as we get off track throughout our lives. He is the BEST GPS system.

Those three months, Jesus and I went round-for-round. I was that little kid having a temper tantrum because I didn't want to humiliate myself on stage. Did it work out in my favor? You guessed it: it didn't.

The day came for me to stand on stage and unveil the deepest parts of my innermost being. As I stood there shaking like Don Knotts it dawned on me that the Holy Spirit was speaking in and through me. Because of my nervousness I said a prayer in my head for the Lord to use me to speak the words needed to bless someone with my testimony. I asked to be used in a way that I had never been used before because even though I was sharing my testimony I needed the words I spoke to penetrate the hearts of the ladies I was standing in front of and speaking to. You see, these women lived in a shelter, had been strung out on drugs or alcohol, been in abusive relationships and/or lived on the street. I didn't feel my story would relate to anyone there because I wasn't strung out on drugs or alcohol, I had been in abusive relationships but I escaped, and I had never lived on the street.

Boy, was I wrong. When the Lord uses you to do a work in the lives of others, He will pull up parts of your past that you tried to bury due to shame, guilt, embarrassment, or you simply wanted to keep those things secret and never wanted anyone to know. Which clearly meant, I was still damaged, still hurting, still in pain, still needing help in all areas, but daily wearing the mask as if life was perfectly fine.

The moment I stood on that stage and said my opening line was the moment I knew I was made for this. Stepping off the stage I had eleven women walk up to me and ask if I would be their mentor. I knew at that moment sharing my testimony was a part of my purpose. Then came sharing my story on more stages and facilitating workshops with more speaking engagements and shortly after, the title idea for a book and coaching business. What was coaching? In 2008, coaching (life coaching) was fairly new and I didn't know what it was or how I could or would implement it into a business.

What was God doing in my life? I had no idea, but I was beginning to enjoy the ride. I was beginning to see Him do things in my life I had only fantasized, cried and prayed about.

So what did I do? I grabbed a three subject notebook and on the first page I wrote the title of the book that kept coming to my mind. I then began to research what coaching was, how to properly speak, what to charge, how to start a business. I went and listened to other well-known speakers to understand if this was something God was calling me to. I needed to be prepared, right? In the meantime, I needed a job; funds were running low and any grown woman would be sick and tired of sleeping on a chaise lounge.

I began to take my mother's advice and read my Word more, pray more, talk to God as if He were my best friend and pour my heart out to Him. I did just that! I had conversations with the Lord as if He and I had been besties for years.

When God works, He works! We don't realize who is watching and listening to us and everything we are doing and saying. That is what was taking place in my life. I had no idea that as I was praying there was someone behind the scenes working and sharing my resume with an organization. I had no idea until I went in the local university where I received my Associate's degree to enroll for my Bachelor's, when my long-time career counselor informed me of what she had done when she learned of my moving back to my hometown. Once I received that call to come into this corporation to interview, then to come in and test, I was nervous. About two weeks passed and I hadn't heard anything. However, during that time, I kept praying and reading my Word, driving through my parents' neighborhood talking with my best friend, letting God know what kind of house I longed for, how I wanted it to look inside and out. Also, I began searching for other jobs until I heard the Lord say, "Wait on me!" I began to stress because I had about $39 dollars in the bank and two teenagers to provide for, clothe and feed. So what did I do? I didn't wait on God; I applied for emergency assistance. Yes, you read right!

Living with my parents, I wanted to repay them and the only way for me to do that was to be the one who purchased and prepared all the food for the household. As we walked through the store, I received a phone call from said corporation giving me an offer and a date for training! I asked her if she had the right number, and as she repeated everything she initially stated, I dropped the phone and screamed with excitement. As I picked the phone back up with tears in my eyes, I shared with her that I'd accept, made note of the start date and training date, when I needed to show up and how we would be traveling for training.

The moment I hung up, the only thing I was able to do was scream and cry! The excitement of what God was doing in the life of this ordinary woman, this single mom, was nothing I was expecting. My father immediately grabbed my and my mother's hands, and in aisle 7 of the grocery store, we stopped and prayed. Yes, prayed! About two weeks later I started my new corporate career at a salary unheard of for someone with only an Associate's degree and no experience.

Further behind the scenes, God was working on others and I hadn't a clue. While I waited on God to work on my behalf for employment I listened more to my beautiful mother as she said I should go and see what I would be pre-approved for to buy a house. I had filed bankruptcy two years prior, however, and everyone told me I would not qualify for a home on my own without a co-signer. The week I started my new corporate position I received a call from the mortgage company I had been working with. The amount they shared I was approved for—hear me when I say not pre-approved, but approved—blew my mind! Why? Because I didn't need a co-signer; God approved me!

Again, another praise break with my parents as we stood in their kitchen.

It took a minute for all of this to sink in; however, once I received the keys to my new home, which was about seven months later, it hit me. Once in my new home, the idea of running and owning a business kept coming to my mind. Within two and a half years, I was able to write my book and start my business as a life coach.

Fast forward 10 years: I am now married to a wonderful man with another little precious person, a certified master coach, certified in five areas, an author, trainer, and speaker with a love for helping other women who feel like their lives are crumbling and falling apart.

My anger at God allowed me to stop, pause and take a step back in order to see what it was He was showing me, and I just didn't understand or wasn't trying to see. I had to realize that I wasn't angry at Him, I was angry at myself for choosing the men that I had chosen. Until I accepted the fact that I needed to wait, that I needed to heal and discover who I was, what I was made of, my value, my worth, and cultivate self-love, I would not be ready to receive love from the right man that was placed on this earth for me.

Although you may be like me, overwhelmed with the many challenges of single motherhood, domestic abuse, being homeless, and sexual assault, there is always a way for the situation to work out when we allow God to lead. I found out there were many great things hidden within me that surfaced when my back was against the wall. Once I allowed those beautiful pieces of my puzzle to come together, I was able to become the woman I was purposed to be. I obtained my Bachelor's degree, started my business, wrote my book, purchased my first home, and continue to rise to the occasion no matter what comes my way. When I look at my life now, I stand in Confidence, Boldness, and Authenticity. I travel and speak from a place of Power and not Pity. I coach women on the road to restoration, from clutter to clarity, allowing them to see how self-discovery will help them cultivate self-love, all while having the opportunity to also discover their zone of genius and monetize it. My past was purposed as a catalyst to provide me the keys to my future, destined for me to operate in my gifts to be the Coach, Trainer, Educator, Speaker, and Author I was called to be today!

**Tammy Wylie**, a committed Jesus-follower, is married to the finest man on the planet (for whom she waited 40 years!). While she's written skits, Bible studies, and devotionals for her churches, *Set Apart and Chosen* marks her first try at writing for a wider audience.

An award-winning public speaker, Tammy holds a Life Coaching Certificate from the Academy of Modern Applied Psychology, a BA (Indiana Wesleyan) and a MA in Math (Ohio State) and the Distinguished Toastmaster (DTM) designation. A lifelong teacher, Tammy believes learning happens in the classroom or the boardroom, on the park bench or in a pew. Seven years of classroom teaching and 28 years of Department of Defense service have provided her ample teaching, coaching, and mentoring opportunities.

Tammy lives in Bowie, Maryland with her favorite hubby. She enjoys listening to and coaching anyone God puts in her path.

Walk the Path ... God's Already Gone Ahead

By Tammy Wylie

We're all on a journey, walking the path laid out for us. Sometimes the pathway is smooth and easy, sometimes it's uphill and challenging, and sometimes it's rocky and rutted and difficult. Some paths seem to be dead ends, but God never leaves us stuck, even when it seems every boulder and rift in the road is trying to stop our progress. My path started that way.

Grandma and Grandpa were old, too old to be raising a pair of preschoolers, but they took us in. Mom and Dad? They kept the boys, but not us two girls. I didn't understand; all I knew was somehow I wasn't one of the kids Mom and Dad wanted. So my little sister and I found ourselves on a farm in Ohio, in the custody of our grandparents. Dad had walked out on Mom, leaving her with us four kids, in Indiana, more than once. Grandpa was so angry that he called the sheriff and swore out a warrant against Dad. We didn't see him for years and wouldn't even have recognized him if he had shown up. I felt rejected, but God had other plans. He wasn't about to abandon me, and He was working to move my feet down His path.

My earliest memory is standing by the playpen where my little sister was fussing. In my four-year-old wisdom, I asked, "Was I this much trouble when I was little?" Already I'd started to see myself as a bother, as a burden to others. That's a hard lesson to forget. Frequently, Grandma would lament that she didn't know what to do with me. I learned to stay out of the house and out of the way. My curiosity and yen to know would find me tramping about the fields with my dog, playing with the barn cats, or reading for hours. I had questions. I wanted to know "why" about everything, and even when I didn't know what would happen, I'd try things, like closing my eyes and letting my dog lead me through the woods so I could feel what it's like to be blind. When I did come back into the house, it was often to criticism -- "You never help your sister with the dishes! Why aren't you ever around to work? You're just so lazy." More hard-to-forget lessons.

Sunday mornings, Aunt Lillian would take us to Sunday School. I remember how grown up I felt the first time I got to stay in the service with the adults instead of going downstairs with the kids. At one point I was chosen to be an acolyte; service would start with me marching down the aisle, lighting each of the candles in the front, before the congregation could begin to sing. I had to sit in the front of the church for the whole service, but I also got to snuff out the candles and march back down the aisle before anyone was allowed to leave. This was my first experience serving in the church, but not the last. Later, I sang in the children's choir. From those early days I was learning to serve, no matter what my gifts might be. Another aunt, Aunt Louise, nurtured my interest in church, the Bible, and God. She bought my first New Testament and taught me the 23rd Psalm. She took me places and gave me books that opened my mind to a broader world. She fed my curiosity, answered my questions, and encouraged me to try new things. She had gone to college to become a nurse; maybe college could be for me someday? God put people like Aunt Louise and Aunt Lillian in my life to show me possibilities and opportunities and to open new paths.

On the farm, my job was to carry the trash down to the barnyard to burn. I would carry a handful of those thick wooden matches with me to the burn barrel. A neighbor boy was with me one day and told me that straw didn't burn. Really? The more I thought about it, the more my curiosity grew. I wanted to know and was willing to try things to learn. The next time I set off to burn the trash I took a few extra matches along. Several of our sheds and outbuildings were filled with straw, so I knelt inside one and struck a match -- the straw flared up, and quickly seemed to go out, shriveled and black, with just a faint trail of smoke winding upward. I tried again, with the same result, and again and yet again. Satisfied that my experiment was complete, I concluded the neighbor boy was right...until the next morning when we awoke to see smoke pouring from the shed. The smoldering straw had continued to burn and had fed upon itself until the whole shed was on fire! Thankfully, we were able to extinguish the flames and save the building, but I learned that day that my curiosity could lead down a dangerous path!

When I was 10, Grandpa became ill -- he would have been 75 or so then. He was hospitalized, and we weren't allowed to visit. As we stood in the parking lot, he waved at us from his hospital room window. I remember him calling down, "I'll be home Saturday." I don't know if he knew what was coming, but Grandpa died that Saturday. This was the first time I'd been touched by death, and I didn't know what to do, how to behave. I hated death and didn't want to acknowledge it at all. This was a path I did not want to walk down.

My path got rockier after that. I was getting older, and sassier, and Grandma was getting older and wearier. I'm sure she loved me, but I don't remember a single tender word -- only directions and criticism. School became a place of encouragement and accomplishment for me. One of my teachers would answer every question I asked, often prefacing her reply with "I know you're a smart girl, so you'll understand this." My sixth grade teacher encouraged me to write an essay for a DAR contest, and I won Honorable Mention. Maybe I did have talents? Maybe I did have something to offer!

We were still on welfare, and I got free lunch at school. In exchange, I worked during recess, washing the trays and silverware in the cafeteria. It was hot and humid work, but I liked stacking the trays into the big machine, then sliding them in to be washed and steamed. The clean silverware was so hot it burned my hands. Even through this, God was weaving lessons into my life: I learned to work hard, to follow directions, to take pleasure in doing a job well. I didn't miss the lunch recess time, because I didn't have very many friends and the only thing I liked doing was playing football with the PE teacher. He always had a gang of boys surrounding him. I played football every chance I got until the day I was hit hard from behind. The boy who hit me glared down at me on the ground and said, "Girls can't play football." I didn't play anymore, but that day I decided I wouldn't let anyone tell me I couldn't do something again!

Near the end of sixth grade, Grandma became ill. My path was about to take a sharp turn. We couldn't live with Grandma any longer. We moved to Indiana to live with Dad, Mom and my two brothers. Some kids might have been excited about getting to live with their "real" family. All I felt was loss. Like the Biblical Ruth, whose circumstances changed because of loss, I went off to a strange land where I didn't know anything about the people, the schools, the expectations -- anything. I didn't have a choice then, but I resolved I wouldn't be a victim of circumstances again. I took refuge in school -- I'd had success there before and found it again. My curiosity and questioning mind led me to love math and Spanish and I made friends with the teachers for those subjects. The language seed, planted way back here in Junior High, would show up again later in my life.

School was what I was good at, and I longed to go to college. I had few role models -- Aunt Louise was the only family member that had ever gone to college -- but I wanted to learn and know and find answers to my questions. And I wasn't afraid to try, even when I didn't know how. Mom helped me get a job at her office and I worked all summer saving my money for tuition. A wonderful elderly couple in our church, the Harveys, had taken an interest in me and on one life-changing day, Mrs. Harvey took me on a college visit to Indiana Wesleyan University. Immediately I sensed in my spirit this was the place for me. That fall I took my first step of independence, moved into the dorm, and never moved back home again. God gave me opportunities to work summers and earn funds for the next semesters. I'm pretty sure the Harveys also helped with funds without me knowing it. God put people like the Harveys in my life to show me possibilities and opportunities, and to help me through some of the challenges along the path.

One summer my path forked -- a mission group was seeking young people to travel to Colombia. My Spanish professor encouraged me, but I was fearful. I didn't know if I could communicate, I didn't know if I could raise the funds, I didn't know if I was "good enough" for a mission trip. But God had given me the curiosity and willingness to try, so I did. God showed up so many times on that trip, and the experience changed the course and direction for the rest of my life-path.

Early in the trip we traveled by canoe to a village with a railway line where we were to board the train. The leader of our group had our tickets in hand but had gone off to help a team member who had taken ill. Suddenly it was time for the train to depart but we didn't have the tickets. The group turned to me for guidance — why they thought I'd know what to do is still a mystery to me! Should we wait for the missionary and our tickets? What if he was on the train and it left without us? Should we board the train? What would happen to us when they found out we didn't have tickets? What should we do? Taking a deep breath, I did what I'd always done — I tried something, even when I didn't know what would happen. We boarded. The train was packed, and I was literally standing on the bottom step in the train car doorway. Clutching my suitcase in one hand, the door railing in the other, I could see the Colombian landscape speeding past, just below my feet. As I perched there precariously in the dark of the evening, I could see through the train car windows that the conductor was making his way down the aisle collecting tickets. My heart beat faster as I prayed and prayed for God to intervene. Just as the conductor reached my step, a hand reached through the crowded train car towards him. In that hand ... my train ticket! Our leader stepped forward and presented the tickets and all was well. Whew! God heard my prayer and He'd been directing my path. I learned that He provides, that He's on the path with me, always, even in the darkest nights in the remotest country, on the lowest step of a speeding train car.

Several days later, in a quiet little village in the hills, we sat on the porch in the cool of the evening. Two small village girls visited, and their bright eyes sparkled while they asked questions of this "gringa," this stranger from another land. One of them sweetly asked, "Tell us a story." I didn't know any stories, especially none in Spanish! But God brought to mind a parable of Jesus -- the lost coin. I told the story slowly and simply, using the vocabulary I knew, and the little girls understood. That night, I was a real missionary, telling others about God's love! On that trip I got a sense of how big the world was and how big God's plans are. I saw that I could play a part in His plan. I didn't know where this new insight would lead, but God was showing me that He could use me to touch other people.

College ended, life continued, with jobs, grad school, new adventures, and marriage to the finest man I've ever met. I could easily conclude I was living "happily ever after." But God had more plans and more for my path! What do you do when you're given a vision that is bigger than you? Shy away, offer excuses like Moses? Or do you try anyway -- if the vision succeeds, you know God did it and He gets the credit. That happened to me. God had plans for me that included another twist in the path.

One Sunday, God sent José to our church in Maryland. He was a small, quiet, kind man from Guatemala. José didn't speak English, so when he arrived, one of the greeters came looking for me. José explained, "I want to be with the people of God." He was at our church services regularly after that, always smiling, friendly, though quiet because of the language problem. We encouraged him to sit with us, and I'd try to translate the sermon in a low voice and whispers. On one occasion I quite happily described to José that Jesus would forgive his fish! Turns out "pescado" (fish) sounds a lot like "pecado" (sin). José didn't laugh at me, but gently supplied the proper word and we pressed on with the sermon.

After a few weeks we began to think about how to help José cope in an English environment. Then, in a vision clearly from God, I began to think, *Who else could we help?* The area around the church was a collage of colors, races, beliefs and nationalities. What if God would let us meet a need for the "next door" neighbors as well as for José? Thus, our English as a Second Language (ESL) ministry was born. Hubby and I set out to understand how we fit into God's vision. We didn't have any experience; we didn't have any funds; we didn't have a plan, but God had given us the sense that He was directing us to do it. We contacted a gracious ESL leader nearby, who invited us to visit her program. This meeting was clearly a God-thing -- she explained how her program ran, she gave us samples of text-books and descriptions of how to assess students, and a host of tips and ideas she'd picked up along the way. She taught us things we didn't even think to ask! Armed with this treasure trove we launched our first 10-week semester of ESL. That first year we had about 20 students. God gave us helpful and kind congregation members to work one-on-one with the students, provide refreshments, or babysit the youngsters. It was a mea-ger start, but the program continued and grew! At the end of our fifth year we reported 102 students from 11 different coun-tries and more than 30 volunteer workers. God took our desire to help one man and turned that into a hundredfold vision. Who else could make such a thing happen? It wasn't our brilliance, or a huge financial donation or a government program; it was God using us as we were available to bring about His plan. Today that ministry continues to reach the neighbors — people who wouldn't normally be drawn into the church arrive weekly to practice English and receive encouragement and fellowship, freely given in the name of Jesus. God put people like José in my life to show me possibilities and opportunities, and to nudge me down the path He had planned.

Since then I've had opportunities to serve in the church and in my workplace in some amazing leadership positions. At church we started a young adult ministry, helping young couples and singles find their places in service and ministry and develop a fellowship that continues today. This fall, my husband and I organized the collection of more than 100 shoebox gifts for kids for a charitable program. At work, I've had a chance to recruit, hire, and train more than 100 eager, young, new employees and get them started in the work world.

I didn't start out to be a trailblazer, but I've come to see that God gave me a curious spirit — one that feels the nudge to go somewhere different, to try something new, to "push that button" just to see what happens! I've learned that God is always with us, and His plans are always good for us (Jeremiah 29:11). Sometimes it's hard to see Him and sometimes it takes years before we recognize His hand at work. I was just a burden, a poor, small-town, lazy welfare girl, abandoned by her parents — not much of an auspicious start! But God (what a powerful phrase!) put people in my life to show me possibilities and opportunities. God STILL has plans for me and is STILL working to move my feet down His path. I can't see around the next bend, but I've learned to trust that He is on the path with me, always.

 **Tishika Taylor-Jackson** is a loving wife, and mother of four children, one of whom is in heaven. She was born and raised in New Orleans, Louisiana. She moved to the Dallas, Texas area as a refugee of Hurricane Katrina in 2005. Since moving there, she started a career in the health care field as an Intravenous Technician. She is also an Independent Paparazzi Jewelry Consultant. She loves 'do-it-yourself' projects and couponing. Since the passing of her son, she has dedicated her life to blessing others in memory of her Angel by using her passion for crafting and couponing to give back. She teaches her children that giving is the greatest gift of grace and to never lose hope. She is grateful God has given her a platform to tell her story. She will continue to inspire people to press forward during the difficult storms in their lives.

Purpose in My Pain

By Tishika Taylor-Jackson

My family became complete in January 2014, when my husband and I were blessed with a beautiful little boy. We each had a daughter from previous relationships—Tyriel (14) and Taylor-Jade (13)—at the time. Many people are unaware that we are a blended family because of the closeness and love we both share for the girls. My husband was elated at the birth of our son because he had always wanted another male in the household. I was excited yet slightly nervous because it had been a while since I had to care for a newborn baby. When I announced my pregnancy to family and friends, I received both criticism and praise for my choice to procreate considering the fact that we had two high school-age daughters. Despite others' concerns, my husband and I were delighted at the chance to be parents again. This was welcoming as we were adjusting to our lives as Texans since relocating from New Orleans in the wake of Hurricane Katrina in 2005.

We named our firstborn son Caleb Elijah Jackson. I will never forget the car ride home from the hospital. It was around the time of the NFL playoffs and he was dressed in a personalized onesie that bore his first name and the logo of the New Orleans Saints (his dad's favorite team). The girls, who were on winter break from school at the time, were both super excited to have their little brother come home from the hospital. Tyriel and Taylor-Jade made amazing big sisters to Caleb. They not only held and played with him but pitched in with diaper changing and bottle feeding. They also never complained about the middle of the night baby crying spells that I'm sure woke them up.

By the end of 2014, we had created so many priceless memories with Caleb. For Easter, he took pictures with real bunnies. He also had a little taste of beignets. During the summer months, he spent a lot of time in his little personal swimming pool as we discovered his love for water. He dressed up as little Batman for a "Boo at the Zoo" event during Halloween. We ended up going back to the zoo the following day to retrieve one of his tennis shoes. He would purposely kick his shoes off and throw them, which is what he did while on the train ride that circles the zoo. For Christmas that year we took him to take pictures with Santa Claus. As Santa chanted 'Ho, ho, ho,' Caleb appeared to be unimpressed and gave him a look of confusion. We were unable to snap a picture with him looking at us, as he was fixated on Santa. Soon after the Santa debacle, we learned that he had a fear of Christmas trees when we put up our tree for the holiday season. He would become terrified at the notion of just touching the tree. This was very funny to my husband and me because he was a very curious child and was always getting into everything but was scared of a Christmas tree. His birthday came less than two weeks after Christmas, so we decided to take him to Chuck E. Cheese to celebrate. I planned on having a huge celebration when he turned two years old, but unbeknownst to me he would never see that age while on earth.

2015 rolled in with us continuing to adjust to having a baby in the house. We took a mini-vacation in June to San Antonio, where we visited Sea World, the Alamo and the Riverwalk. In

July, my relatives from New Orleans had planned on visiting me in Arlington for our annual family vacation. Since I'd relocated there after Hurricane Katrina, a host of my family members would visit every year in July and would enjoy some of the many attractions the Dallas/Fort Worth metroplex had to offer. Around the Fourth of July is when I would become eager, knowing my family would be there soon.

Friday, July 17 started off like any other weekday morning. After he was fully dressed, Caleb walked across the hall and burst into his sister's bedroom and proceeded to annoy her.

Depending on her mood that morning she would ignore him or entertain his shenanigans until it was time to fix breakfast. Taylor-Jade fixed breakfast every morning for her brother. He loved to sit in his high chair and watch Barney as he ate. My brother would come home from working a graveyard shift and play with Caleb before he left for school. The whole house was excited because it was Friday: my last day of work and my daughter's last day of the summer science program she attended before vacation began. I got my purse and kissed Caleb on the forehead before I took Taylor-Jade to science camp while my husband took Caleb to school. He yelled, "Bye Mommy" so loud and with a screeching voice. This was the last time I saw my child alive.

I made it to work but my mind remained in vacation mode, so I was just ready for the day to be over. We had just gotten paid and I didn't have a lot of work scheduled; it seemed like it was the perfect day leading up to vacation. My phone was face down on my desk on vibrate to prevent me from getting distracted. After a while I realized I had missed two phone calls from a number I didn't recognize. A few minutes after missing those calls, my desk phone rang. It was our city's fire department. They asked if I was the parent of Caleb Jackson. I responded with a frantic

"YES." The man on the phone said there had been a choking incident with my son, so I panicked and asked if he was okay. They
refused to give me any information over the phone. I was told
what hospital to meet them at. I called my husband and asked
him to leave and meet me there. I remember running to my
manager's office and saying, "I must leave; something is wrong
with my baby." I grabbed my purse and ran to my car; I burst out
the door so fast I hurt my wrist. I called my husband back and
told him I was en route to the hospital. I was crying hysterically.
I kept saying, "God, please let him be okay." I asked my husband
to please call me as soon as he got there and let me know he
was okay. I worked a few minutes from the hospital. I decided to
call my mother, but she didn't pick up the phone. I immediately
dialed my auntie Pat's number. I still was crying and having a
panic attack. She kept saying, "Shika, Shika, please try and calm
down. Please tell me what's wrong." I told her the heartbreaking
call I got about my son, but no one would talk to me and give me
information over the phone about his condition. She began to
pray for him. She kept trying to calm my nerves because I was
driving so fast and crying on the interstate. I talked to my aunt
until I pulled in the parking lot of the hospital. It was a very pretty,
sunny day outside. I remember telling her, "Something is wrong
because Ronald didn't call me back." I knew he worked only fifteen minutes from the hospital. I should have heard something
by then. I told Aunt Pat I would call her as soon as I found something out. I tried calling my husband, but I didn't get an answer.
I walked in the Emergency Room doors and was greeted by the
hospital Chaplain. I saw the Bible in his hand, and I screamed and
fell to my knees. I ran in the hospital and turned to the left and
saw my baby lying in a bed with no machines attached to him. I
was stopped by several nurses and police officers from going in
the room. I was fighting, cussing, screaming, "Please bring him

back to me." I begged them to allow me to hold him one more time. The officer on duty told me if I calmed down, they would allow me some time with him before they came to pick up his body. I remember sitting in the room next to my husband, holding our son. I sang his favorite song, prayed over him, talked to him, and squeezed him so tight. It looked like he was peacefully sleeping. They moved me into a small room with my husband. I started vomiting everywhere. They immediately started calling all our close family members. I ended up being admitted into the hospital because of the drastic change in my mental and physical health. I remember sitting in the hospital bed surrounded by family and friends. I just couldn't stop the tears from flowing. I wasn't sure how I was going to break the news to our daughters. This was the worst day of my life. I had to figure out how to grieve and be strong for our children.

My Pastor and Bishop met us at a relative's house once I was discharged from the hospital. I was still in a state of shock. I kept asking why did this happen to me? Why are we being punished? I felt so guilty because I was at work when everything happened. I had so many unanswered questions and anger started setting in. I was so angry at God because I wasn't ready to let my baby boy go. I had no idea how to plan a funeral. I am thankful for our church family because they made sure everything was taken care of. All we had to do was make major decisions no parent wants to talk about. I vaguely remember the day of my sweet angel's funeral. However, I do remember finding the strength to stand next to my daughters as they spoke their final words to their brother. We laid him to rest and had a beautiful fellowship afterwards. I still was in a state of shock and denial. It was time for us to find our new normal, but how was I supposed to do that?

One day I drove myself to a jailhouse and asked them to arrest me. I told them I was a bad mother for not protecting my child.

I drove myself there and was in the parking lot, crying uncontrollably and having an anxiety attack. I called my closest friends and told them where I was and to come get my car and bring it home. I remember Shay arriving at the station. She saw me sitting on the bench waiting to speak with the officers. She went up to the window and I still have no idea what she told them. Immediately two officers (male and female) came and sat with me. They asked me a few questions. I told them a mother should never have to bury her child. Even though my baby's death was an accident and I wasn't with him when it happened, I didn't deserve to be free because I failed to protect him as a parent. The female officer started crying because she then realized I was suffering from survivor's guilt. They were both very compassionate and allowed me to have my moment and share videos and pictures of Caleb with them. Of course, they told me I was always welcome to come to talk to an officer if I needed to.

The first year after the passing of my son was the hardest for my family, for we had no desire to celebrate anything. I was afraid to be around small children, especially little boys, so I isolated myself from the outside world. I was tired of hearing people tell me my child was in a better place and he wouldn't want me to be sad. By then I had entered a deep, dark depression stage in my life. I had lost all hope and wanted to leave Earth to be with my son. I visited his grave every day because I felt that is what a mother was supposed to do. I kept trying to find ways to include him in all my day-to-day decisions. I was full of so much guilt on so many levels. Life had gone on for everyone but me. How was I supposed to live without my sweet Caleb? I didn't feel deserving at all. My husband helped find me some professional help because I seemed to be stuck in the anger and denial stage of grief. I was even angry at my husband because he was living and functioning so well in society. At least that was my perception of everything. He told me that Caleb would forever be in our hearts and we must find a way to live for our children here on earth. I never was able to move back into the home we shared with Caleb. My husband had to pack up the whole house by himself, because I couldn't step foot back in there. I started writing all my thoughts down and being honest about my feelings to the world. I never sugar-coated or Photoshopped my feelings to anyone. I attended several grief classes, and this really helped me learn I was not alone on this journey. It opened my eyes to a whole new world of grieving families. Life continued, but my heart was stuck in 2015.

I even got evaluated at a mental institution and had to see a psychiatrist. I liked to self-inflict pain to redirect the pain in my heart. I was told there really wasn't a cure for a grieving mom and they put me on a lot of medications to help me function normally in society. I'm not sure why I am telling you this, but I wish people would stop and ask themselves, "What child can I live without?" Living as a grieving mom is not as easy as people make it seem.

Caleb was a very happy baby. He touched so many hearts in such a short time. I didn't want my child to be forgotten about and decided to do things in the community in honor of him. I began donating school supplies, having coat drives, toy drives, and making care packages, all in memory of my son. I had such amazing support from so many friends, family, and the entire community. It brought me so much joy to bless others in honor of my Angel son. This helped me redirect some of my grief into a positive situation. I began living and not existing in life again. I took baby steps into functioning in society. I have learned not to take things people say so personally. Most of the time someone is giving advice to a grieving parent, they really have no clue what to say. They mean well, the majority of the time. I find it easier to talk to other grieving parents.

Even during my storm, I still found a way to lean on God and have trust in my faith. Some days seem to be harder than others, but I am alive. I never thought I would say this, but I got pregnant with another boy. My emotions and feelings were all over the place. My initial feeling was fear because I felt I had already let down one child. I kept wondering why God would pick me to be a mother of another son after He had taken one? Some people were excited because they said I could stop obsessing over keeping Caleb's memory alive. Needless to say, I had to remove a lot of unnecessary ignorance from my life. Just because we are having a son, this doesn't erase or replace the pain and/or love we have for Caleb. I was an emotional wreck the whole pregnancy. I fell back into a deeper depression because of my fear of not being the perfect mom. The further along onto the pregnancy the more I felt anxious and scared. My husband was elated to find out we were having another son. He had another opportunity to play football or basketball with his son. Also, he would get to name this baby because he allowed me to name Caleb. What many don't know is Josiah was the name my husband wanted to give to Caleb initially. I told him he could name our second son. I never believed I'd have another little boy. It was very ironic because "Josiah" means "God heals." This was the perfect name for our rainbow baby. Josiah is our rainbow because he came to us after a major storm in our lives. HE gave us a new purpose for living. I began pressing forward in my grief in a much healthier way. It was okay for me to mourn the loss of one child and prepare to welcome another. It was hard at first looking at baby boy things in the stores, but I took baby steps. I was grateful for the people who made sacrifices to help me on my healing journey.

I never knew I would be able to comfortably talk about my grief journey that I am still walking in. I have strengthened my relationship with God. I never thought I would be able to smile and cry happy tears. I genuinely believe Josiah was heaven-sent and handpicked by his brother Caleb. He gives me so much hope, joy, happiness, and brought wholeness to my world. I successfully delivered a beautiful baby boy in the beginning of the year. My boys have so much in common. I am watching Josiah grow before my eyes and he reminds me so much of his brother. The physical similarities are amazing. I hear the word "ma ma," and it warms my heart. I never thought I would ever be able to bring another child into this world. I had allowed grief and depression to consume my every thought and move in life. I had reached the lowest point ever in my life and lost all hope. I am grateful for the spiritual and professional help I have received over the years. It is possible to find happiness even in my darkest hour. I may not be the same person I used to be, but I did survive being a prisoner of my own guilty mind.

**Dr. Tasheka L. Green**, servant leader, educator, inspirational speaker, transformational coach, six-time author, entrepreneur, philanthropist, and talk show host, is the Founder, President, and Chief Executive Officer of To Everything There is a Season, Inc. Her innovative coaching techniques influence personal, professional development and organizational change. She leads with a focus to support individuals and organizations in identifying their purpose. Dr. Green's work garnered her a feature in the Harvard University School of Education, HarvardX Course, Introduction to Data Wise: A Collaborative Process to Improve Learning & Teaching.

A scholarly and virtuous woman, her extraordinary faith, vision, talents, presence, and accomplishments have allowed her to obtain a plethora of recognitions and awards. Dr. Green is an example of when preparation meets opportunity, the end result is success. She loves God and radiates with the joy of the Lord.

Dr. Green is married to William Z. Green Sr, and they have three beautiful children, Marquis (21), Mikayla (8), and William Jr. (6).

Submit to the Choosing

By Dr. Tasheka L. Green

"Without faith it is impossible to please God" (Hebrews 11:6, NIV). One act of faith will please God, change your entire life and release you into the plan of God. Often, it is our unbelief, our doubts, our fears, that hold us back from what God has for us. We want to control life's situations, but God is requiring us to let go and trust Him with our entire life. I can speak from this principle directly because I was that person who tried to control so much of my life, but the day came when I had no other choice but to let go and let God be Lord in and over my life and walk in a place called chosen and set apart.

My life was violently disrupted without my permission. The one thing that I had most feared showed up in my life on July 19, 2018. I have always been a goal-oriented, determined woman who persevered, endured, and never stopped until I reached my goals. Once I reached one goal, I knew there was more for me to do, so I would pursue and move in an onward progression. It seemed as though there was always a pulling, a zeal, a passion to help masses of people to discover the best within themselves. In my career, I have always been successful and ensured that everyone and everything attached to me achieved greatness too. Along my journey, and in my endeavors to pursue greatness, I joined an organization that needed improvement with its organizational structure and effectiveness. I entered into this organization at an executive level position with a purpose mindset rather than a job or career mindset. My primary mission was to influence and impact change in everyone's life that I met, taught, served and helped. I committed to the calling of being a transformational servant leader by educating, serving, helping, and loving others to greatness.

"God chooses you and sets you apart, separating and making you different. Calling you out of a crowd from everyone else, to fulfill the plans He created for you. Plans to prosper you and not to harm you, plans to give you hope and a future" (Jeremiah 29:11, NIV). "For many are invited, but a few are chosen" (Matthew 22:14, NIV) to fulfill the acceptable desired plan that God has designated for you, which is a life of victories, miracles, wisdom, mysteries, opportunities, and favor. The choosing is not for you, but for God to get all the glory out of your life. Your response to the choosing will determine the outcome. When you are chosen by God, you are directly the purpose of His choice or His divine favor. God could have chosen anyone else, but He chose you, because He saw something great in you before you even entered your mother's womb. The conception of who you are began in the mind of God, and His choosing of you birthed you into a place called God's purpose. Now that you are chosen and set apart, there is a greater expectation of you for God's kindness, generosity, and favor.

"For it is in Him we live, move and have our being" (Acts 17:28, NIV). Your story, your life, my story, my life, the process you have been through will testify of God's goodness and bring you to an unexpected end. The pain will declare God's love and position you in the place that He has chosen for you. Great is God's faithfulness toward us. When God chooses us and sets us apart, there are greater expectations that we have to fulfill. "From everyone who has been given much, much will be demanded; and from the one who has been entrusted with much, much more will be asked" (Luke 12:48, NIV).

When you are chosen and set apart, you may feel as though you are in an isolated place. You may be alone, but you will never be lonely. God is in the midst and right there with you. God will walk with you, talk with you, and tell you that you are His own. "For God's word is a lamp unto your foot, and a light unto your path" (Psalm 119:105); and "goodness and love" (Psalm 23:6, NIV) are following you all the days of your life. Just stay focused on the light and walk in the direction in which God has ordered, listen to His voice, and be obedient to the choosing.

During my tenure with this organization, there were several changes which occurred that in turn impacted my career. On July 19, 2018, I was given notice that my position would be eliminated in 45 days. In a ten-minute executive meeting, I was informed that eighteen years of my career would be coming to an end in 45 days. I sat still in disbelief, trying to maintain my focus, but all I could think of was my family and how this impacted all of us. As I walked out of the meeting and moved quickly to my car, I began to silently weep, because life had just changed that very moment. I was concerned about where I was going to sleep, what I was going to eat, and what was going to happen. For God's word said, "And my God will meet all your needs according to the riches of his glory in Christ Jesus" (Philippians 4:19, NIV). Then I recalled all that God had done prior to this day. The entire year, God had me studying and meditating on Matthew 6:25-34, which speaks on not worrying about life's matters, what you will eat or drink; or about your body, what you will wear, for God already knows what we need. If it is a need, God will supply it, make a way, or change the situation. In my weeping, I knew in my heart that God had me covered, and that He would not let the weapon that was formed prosper.

During this time, I reapplied and interviewed for the position in which I currently served within the organization. The next day I received a call and heard these words: "You were not chosen." I sat back in the chair, inhaled, exhaled and said, "Thank you, Jesus!" And then I remembered that many are called, but a few are chosen, and the choosing can only come from one person, and that is God. For eighteen years, I had committed to the calling, but now I had to reposition myself, align my life, and submit to the choosing. In all my getting, I had to get understanding, and know that I was chosen for this, and I would not be broken or defeated.

With that being said, I was faced with what at first looked like an obstacle. However, when I looked again, my vision showed an opportunity. The circumstances presented before me made it possible to do something. I could either act by submitting to the choosing, fulfilling the purpose, and walk in a direction of progress and advancement, or react by responding and becoming subjected to the obstacle.

Note to self: "When you are faced with an obstacle, look at it as an opportunity. Train your eye to see past the problem and look toward the future. Reinvent yourself, know who you are and your worth, be clear about your purpose, submit to the choosing, and live your best life."

When you are faced with an obstacle, look at it as an opportunity for you to learn, grow, make a greater impact, and change your circumstance for the better. The best opportunities are the ones you create. Whatever you are faced with, just know opportunity may cost; you may have to give up something to acquire or achieve something else, but it leads to success. Do not miss out on the opportunity because you are so focused on the obstacle. Therefore, pick up your paintbrush, take out your canvas and finish your masterpiece. The masterpiece is what God has chosen you to fulfill.

I am an example of when preparation meets opportunity it leads to success. The journey I took to get here was chosen and ordered by God. It led me to a place called peace, joy, contentment, and love. After being eliminated from my position and not chosen by man, God placed me in a place called more than enough. All I had to do was to show up with an expectation of gratitude, and let God do the rest. Today, I celebrate that I am the Founder, President, and Chief Executive Officer of To Everything There Is A Season, Inc., "where we turn dreams into a vision, and your vision into a reality." All of this was the choosing which God had already designed for my life; all I had to do was believe, seek, and then I could achieve.

Therefore, my friends, I leave you with this thought…How many of you have had a door that recently or abruptly closed in your life? Do you know that God has chosen you and will lead you out of whatever state you are in? When God closes that door in your life, be certain and know God is your exodus, your way out. When the door closes what will you do? Will you stand behind the closed door, try to find another way around it, or trust God and let Him lead you?

My friends, let God lead you, follow Him, and submit to the choosing. When one door closes, God will open multiple doors of great opportunities, which no one can shut. Open doors are set before you. Therefore ask, and if it is according to God's will it will be given to you. Seek, and wait on God to respond; His sheep know His voice. Then knock, and God will open the door, so you can walk through it. This time when you look back the only thing following you is goodness and love all the days of your life. Open doors are set before you, because you have been chosen and set apart. Walk through the doors to which God leads you.

It's your season; go and live a purposeful life.

Pamala Mintz is a successful mother of 3 children, Tiara, Brandon, and Joshua, and the grandmother of 1, London. She graduated from Coppin State University in 2008 with a Bachelor of Arts in English/Communications and graduated from the University of Baltimore with a Master of Science in Health Systems Management in 2013. Pamala is currently pursuing her PhD in Health Care Administration at Capella University.

Pamala has authored and published four books. She is a member of Restoration International Worship Center, under the leadership of Bishop Marvin Denson and Lady Michele Denson. She also serves as Chair of the Board of Directors for the Family Health Centers of Baltimore. Pamala is currently engaged to the love of her life, Mgary Williams.

For more information visit: www.pammintz.com

When God Pushes Pause

By Pamela Mintz

What happens when you are just living? You are living ... doing your thing! You are happy, successful and prosperous. You have accepted the fact that you are set apart and chosen! You are highly favored! You are blessed! You are following God, so you think, and then suddenly He presses pause. What do you do now? There is no how-to book to tell you what to do. You pray, fast, and read your scriptures, but nothing changes. So what do you do when God pushes **PAUSE**?

What is a **PAUSE**? According to Webster's dictionary, a **PAUSE** is a temporary stop in action or an interruption. It's a stop with a deadline but it is enough to make you feel stagnant. It's enough for you to wonder if you will ever get out of the present situation. It's enough for you to reconsider all your actions. Each **PAUSE** has a lesson and it's up to you to grasp it as soon as possible or risk repeating it until you pass the test. Is the **PAUSE** a test? Possibly, but no one can give you an answer key and you can't study for it. The funny part is God gives you the test before the lesson is taught. Ironically, you are prepared for a test that you didn't expect. It's like a pop quiz. You were given the information to study, but you didn't take it seriously. You thought you had time.

Obedience is better than sacrifice. Sounds like a cliché, right? But it's so true. How many times can one person be labeled as hardheaded? Based on my experiences, a lot! Time after time, God was pressing pause in my life and I kept wondering why! WHY! WHY! WHY!

My story started when I was a little girl. When I was eight or nine, my mother and godmother took me to Disney World in Florida. I was walking through Magic Kingdom and came upon the castle. It was so pretty and magical. At that very moment, I wondered if I would grow up and marry a Prince. Doesn't every little girl dream of her Prince Charming? You imagine a tall, dark and handsome man who sweeps you off your feet. You never in a million years imagine kissing thousands of frogs to find him. You never think that dream won't happen exactly like you dreamed it, right? You never imagine that you would experience God at such a young age either, right?

Every Sunday, I was in Sunday School and church ALL day at the Baptist Church with my grandmother, Gladys. She was a Trustee, but she was also a Mother at the church. She was a part of the Pastor's Aide. She fixed the communion table and she cooked and served dinner after morning service. So, of course, where was I? You guessed it! I was alongside her every time the church door opened, I ushered. I presided over services. I sang in the choir. I sang solos. I cleaned the church. I was a church kid. My childhood was uneventful until I turned 16. My absent father showed up, trying to parent, and I became a rebellious teenager. Struggling with low self-esteem issues, I decided the only way I could have a pretty baby was to find a baby daddy that was tall, light-skinned and had curly hair. Why was I even considering being a teenage mother? After all, I was a church kid; I knew right from wrong. I knew I wasn't ready to be a mother. Consequently, I became a teenage mother - **PAUSE!!!!**

The first **PAUSE** occurred in my senior year of high school. Two weeks after graduation, I had my first child. I had a beautiful baby girl. I knew nothing about motherhood. Actually, I didn't even like dolls so what would I do with a baby? This **PAUSE** was the first but certainly wasn't going to be the last. During this pause, my best friend, Janean, had a massive heart attack and died. Not only was I adapting to being a new mother but I also had to deal with a death. My emotions were all over the place. How could God do this to me? WHY! WHY! WHY!

Thankfully that "**PAUSE**" didn't last long. I entered college immediately the summer after high school. Even though, I had a four-month-old and my best friend had died, I was determined to get back in the saddle and still be great. Besides, I was a church kid and I was taught that I was set apart and chosen. God forgave me, so life must go on. College was going great until I met a "counterfeit" Prince Charming! We went to the store one day and he bought me a ring and proposed. I said yes. I said yes to the devil. Two weeks after I said I do, he punched me in my face! **PAUSE**! This can't be happening! Another **PAUSE**! For way too long, I endured physical, mental and sexual abuse at the hands of a "counterfeit" Prince Charming! He beat me! He punched me! He sexually raped me with a gun! WHY! WHY! WHY!

I knew that this **PAUSE** was destined to kill me! It appeared that everyone was against me, even my own family. The most interesting aspect of this **PAUSE** was I sought God to help me and it seemed like He was ignoring me. One Sunday morning after church was the day, this "counterfeit" Prince Charming pulled out his 9mm gun to take my life. He loaded it and aimed it right at my face in front of my three-year old daughter. Only grace and mercy saved me that day. I stood strong looking down the barrel of that gun, knowing my life was over. That **PAUSE** nearly killed me! Again, WHY! WHY! WHY!

Life continued, and I graduated with my Bachelor of Arts degree when my daughter (my first **PAUSE**) graduated high school. Then I graduated with my Master of Science degree when my first **PAUSE** graduated with her Bachelor of Science degree. Imagine that! The **PAUSE** that appeared to be a lesson was a blessing that pushed me to greatness. Now this is how my life should be going!

I am SET APART and CHOSEN!
Life was looking up! I was beginning to live out my dreams. I lost over 60 pounds and was getting healthier. I had written and published two books. I was traveling around the United States doing book signings. My book was growing a great fan base. I was selling books and t-shirts through my newly formed business. I hosted my first book event and authors traveled from as far as California to participate. I was beginning to co-host my first radio show. Our audience was growing by leaps and bounds. I was living the way I should have years ago! I competed in a beauty pageant. Not only did I compete but I won best overall interview. Can you believe the girl who grew up with low self-esteem issues competed in a beauty pageant? I was confident, beautiful and living my dreams.

I am SET APART and CHOSEN!
Then I heard five dreadful words ... "You need a heart transplant!"

PAUSE!
Not again! Not now! My life is finally on track and now this! All right God, I survived every trial up until this point. Why now? I have a successful radio show. I am a published author. I have competed in a beauty pageant despite my self-esteem

issues. This was the ultimate **PAUSE**! A major body organ is literally dying with no warning. God, you got jokes! This is a joke, right? NO RESPONSE!

Now the tears were flowing because I can't control this. I can't change this. Only you can get me through this one. Lead me! Guide me! Proverbs 3:5-6 reminds me to trust you and that you are directing my path. I'm scared! This "**PAUSE**" is a hard stop! Are you serious? You can't be serious!

Now I'm sure you are wondering why in the world is she talking to God like that? God made me! He knew this moment would come! He knew I would question him! He knew I would be angry! He knew I would wonder why! All my questions, anger, and frustration would not stop his will. Either I would die or he would heal me! It was now totally up to me to believe and trust God or not!

As the "**PAUSE**" continued, I was placed on 17 different pills a day for survival. I was diagnosed with a left ventricle blood clot (located in the widow maker - low percentage of survival), 24% pumping heart, and uncontrolled diabetes. It looked very grim. I wore a life vest 24 hours a day in case my heart stopped. I was now in a wheelchair. I was only allowed to walk to the bathroom and back to bed. My color was leaving my body. I had visitors around the clock as my mother took care of me.

I heard a small voice say, "Get a second opinion!" I sought out another specialist. On my first visit with her, she told me there was no rush to get a transplant. She wanted to try a new regimen of pills. Finally, I began to see light at the end of the tunnel. Three months later, I had another echocardiogram and my heart was up to 35%. Three more months later, I was up to 50%. This was rare. My heart was literally healing itself. Thank God!

God's got jokes! In the middle of the "**PAUSE**," I met a man. Right! Who would want to date a sick woman who could possibly die? You missed it! I said I met a MAN, not a boy, not a friend with benefits, not somebody's son ... A MAN! During our first conversation, we talked for five hours. Our second conversation lasted five hours too. He wanted nothing from me but to help me heal. A friendship was birthed that led to a date. Our first date was a picnic in the park with a gourmet meal cooked by his hands! Whew! A handsome, charming man that can cook! God, you really got jokes! During our first date, he sang to me in the most melodic voice I had ever heard. He sang "I Dreamed You" by Anastacia. I cried.

We started dating and he took care of me. God, during the greatest **PAUSE** in my life, sent me my Prince Charming. He sent me the man I dreamed about as a little girl. He sent the man after I endured low self-esteem, domestic violence, teenage pregnancy, and now a health challenge.

My life is now looking up. My health is getting better.

It took all those things happening for the man of my dreams to find me.

Psalm 27:5

For in the day of trouble he will

keep me safe in his dwelling;

he will hide me in the shelter of

his sacred tent and set me high

upon a rock.

Kendra Randall, Esquire is an Attorney, Entrepreneur, Professor and Community Servant who has devoted her life to advocacy and empowerment of women and children. As an attorney, Kendra has garnered success in civil litigation, family law, child welfare, and ethics for attorneys and judges. She was the Project Manager for her prior law firm's multi-million-dollar government contracts. In 2008, Kendra co-founded A Step Closer Foundation, Inc. (ASCF), a 501(c)(3) non-profit organization, whose mission is to take children a step closer to their destiny. Kendra is the visionary for She Matters, an initiative of ASCF, which hosts life-changing programs that develop, inspire and showcase female accomplishments, including conferences, award ceremonies, summits and business/leadership camps. Thousands have been impacted by attending She Matters events. In addition to She Matters, ASCF enhanced young men's lives through the He Matters: Power of One Program. ASCF also has initiatives to assist foster children, including holiday parties and Trash Bags to Travel Bags. Kendra's current focus is producing a documentary through her company, Her Communications, LLC and developing TV for Girls. Kendra has received numerous awards, as well as local and national media coverage, for her work and community service. She's most thankful to God for the opportunities to minister and mother two beautiful children. Kendra Randall, Esq. COO Her Communications, LLC herinfo@hercommunications.com

Healing the Girl Within

By Kendra Randall

When I was young (I think around nine), my mother was in our basement and I was standing on the steps. I don't remember what I did (or probably said, knowing me), but what I will never forget is that she said. "You're a demon!" In childhood you have those transformational moments that cause you to go back to that exact date and time. You never forget how you felt, how it changed you. You could almost cry like it just happened again.

Fast forward to the summer of 2016. My mom and I had just thrown our annual Fourth of July picnic—great food, DJ, crabs. Everyone had a fun time. While I was maneuvering containers in her refrigerator, I heard my mother yell a derogatory remark to me about how I was arranging the containers. This was in front of our guests. It sent a bone-chilling nerve through my body, and I knew something changed in me. It wasn't as if my mom hadn't yelled at me before. It wasn't as if she hadn't embarrassed me in front of people before. It wasn't as if she hadn't belittled me before, but this time just felt different. This was another life-changing experience, but this time I was forty-seven, and my mom was sixty-five.

Just a few months earlier, I went to Panera Bread to meet my law partner of fifteen years—business partner, co-founder of my nonprofit organization, and godmother to my daughter—for our weekly business meeting on Wednesday. We had been meeting every Wednesday for years and years. We made critical decisions, disagreed, created new approaches to business, discussed personal problems, and addressed all business matters each week. That day was no different, until it was.

"Remember how I told you last year that I felt like I was under water?" my partner asked.

"Yes," I replied.

"I know we both said we don't want to practice law forever, but I don't want to do it anymore, so we will have to close the firm. I'm sorry... The fast I just finished gave me clarity."

"Okay," I said.

I didn't know what else to say. There was an unknown space. I'd been in business with her for over fifteen years through ups, downs, turmoil, and victories, but this was something I could not talk to *her* about because *she* was the problem. I had to address it alone.

She was right; I'd always known I didn't want to practice law forever, but I don't think I would have done it that way. What about my kids? How would I care for them? Would I get a job? They no longer had a legacy business to walk into. I was imagining how my life would change professionally and socially; she and her family were like family to me. My kids had been used to a lifestyle of trips, activities, and eating out sometimes. Would we still do these things? If I got a job, I wouldn't have the same flexibility I had to attend their school events. Maybe I could finally move forward in the business I had wanted to start since 2007.

"Okay." I needed to leave, and I entered the cloud I would be walking in for weeks and months to come.

Although I thought I was putting up a good façade despite my feelings and uncertainty, someone noticed the cloud a week or so later and asked if I was okay.

I replied, "I'm making a career change."

He said, "Hey, I need some hours to get certified in career coaching. Do you want to come have a few sessions pro bono?"

"Sure, I could use that."

I could use career coaching, that's for sure. I didn't know what to do. I was a little mad at myself because I normally knew what to do. *Keep it moving* were my famous words. But why couldn't I move? Why couldn't I just come up with a new plan like I always did? Why couldn't I move? Didn't I realize I was a divorced mother of two wonderful children? They needed health care. They needed food. *Why couldn't I move?*

It turned out that the career coach getting his hours was more than I bargained for. He started asking questions about my childhood. I was getting uncomfortable. "Why did your parents divorce?" I was feeling a little insulted. (I thought this was career coaching; why was he in my personal business? I didn't know if I could do this.) Didn't he understand I needed to figure out my professional life, so I could get some money and help my kids? Didn't he know I had two businesses and co-founded a nonprofit to take children a step closer to their destiny? Despite my childhood, being called a demon and the other negativities from my mom, I overcame that stuff, went to law school, and had dedicated my life to empowering children. Can we just get on with this?

"So why do you think you're so passionate about helping children?" he asked.

"I don't know. I've just always loved kids." I paused, thought, and welled up in emotion I didn't know was there. "I guess I don't want kids to hurt like me. I want them to still have hope, no matter what they're going through. I want them to know they can make it no matter what. I want them to be exposed to things I wasn't exposed to and people like me who care and can help them," I said through my tears. He had tissues; I guess crying was a part of career coaching. I did not go there to be that vulnerable and share my painful truths. CAREER COACHING, PLEASE!?!?

I couldn't tell him that she left me outside overnight to sleep in the leaves under our back porch while my dad worked overnight. I couldn't tell him I was beaten, bruised, and scratched (with the laws today, I would have been one of the foster children I endeavored to help and advocate for). I couldn't tell him I didn't like myself growing up, and when I was twelve, I put a knife to my chest because I wanted to kill myself.

I guess I did not need to tell him because maybe he sensed the other things or heard enough to say, "That's great you do those things for kids, *but* who's going to heal Little Kendra? Who's going to help you?" I cried some more and used up more and more tissues. I hadn't thought about her. I didn't really realize she existed. I did not know she needed to be healed. See, I'd done so much for people. See, I was a good person. See, I was a Christian. See, I was a lawyer. See, I was a role model who did conferences for kids, award ceremonies for kids, camps for kids, summits. See, I was a leader in local and national bar associations with top lawyers in my field. See, I was president of my Jack & Jill chapter. See, I'd won more awards than I can remember due to my work and community service. See! See! See? Why couldn't he see I was just fine? Because I wasn't. Despite all those accolades, I wasn't fine. I gathered myself together and left my "career coaching" session.

Meeting Little Kendra

Days and weeks after the session, I could not stop thinking about Little Kendra. What did she need? Could I help her? Did I want to try?

So one weekend while my kids were with their dad, I was all alone. It was late at night and dark. The TV was off. I woke up in the middle of the night and sat up in my bed looking straight ahead. Little Kendra came to me. I began to feel emotional because I knew I had to talk to her. This time I started crying, sobbing even. It took some time before I could talk to Little Kendra. Nervously, I gathered up the nerve/strength to talk to her. I told her that *she mattered,* just like I have told many of "my kids" over the years. I told her that her mom was not perfect; no one is. I acknowledged the pain she had gone through and witnessed to her she would make it through. That God had great things in store for her. She had a purpose; all the pain and negativity were not going to hinder her. It got easier to talk to Little Kendra. I told her she could be anything she wanted to be and that she still had a lot to be thankful for.

I helped her remember her mom was a teenage parent who made the tough decision to keep her and had to go to high school embarrassed and teased, but she kept her. I told her that her mom had her own unresolved childhood pain—her dad was a "rolling stone" and left them (my mom, her four siblings, and their mother) and moved to New York. I told her a family history of mental illness did not doom her; there was no need to fear. Little Kendra always felt there was something else that happened to her mom, some kind of abuse, that caused her to lash out the way she did. I told Little Kendra it was okay she didn't know; she didn't need to know everything. She was not responsible for her mom's pain. It wasn't her fault. She was just a child. It was not her fault her mom missed out on enjoying her late teenage years and twenties because she was caring for Little Kendra. It was not her fault that her mom was jealous of her bond with her paternal grandmother, the only person Little Kendra felt had unconditional love for her, the reason she did not kill herself at age twelve, the one who made her feel special. That love is why Little Kendra survived, despite the pain. I told her she should appreciate the fact that her mom was there every day and did the best she could with what she had.

I saw the vision of Little Kendra; she started to smile. I felt her pain start to leave me.

A bit of peace started creeping in. Something was opening on the inside; it was like air. I felt lighter. Little Kendra was healed and absorbed into Big Kendra. I realized everything that happened in my childhood wasn't my fault, and that I was the child. Just as my children aren't responsible for my pain, I was not responsible for my mother's pain. Despite the negativities, I could appreciate the good things my mother did for me and love her, nonetheless.

Finally, I paid the price to be free. It was worth every thought, every memory, every bit of analysis, every prayer, every heart-break, sorrow, every tear, and every word uttered to Little Kendra to help heal her pain. I was now okay to embrace the whole me, love me completely, and advocate for myself as I had done for so many others over the years.

New Kendra, New Solutions

"I'll get the hot dogs, sausages, rolls; I will make the kabobs and pasta salad again. You know what, Mom? I would like to have a DJ this year for the cookout. I think that would be a great addition. What do you think?" I asked in preparation for the big Fourth of July shindig.

"Fine with me," said my mom.

DJ, it is. I was excited. This was going to be the best one yet! And everything was great. People enjoyed the crabs, fresh fried fish, line dancing, games, festive atmosphere, camaraderie—fun for young and old. This was one to be remembered, and I was proud until...

Until she yelled at me while I was kneeling on the floor at her refrigerator. I don't know if it was because I was the height of

Little Kendra again, but I felt her pain come back. (No, she can't come back. She's healed, right?)

"Mom, don't yell at me!"

"I will yell at you if you're not doing right! This is *my* house!"

Oh, Little Kendra heard that phrase many times before. This time, though, Big Kendra had somewhere to go. She had her own house.

"Time to go, guys," Big Kendra told her kids. "Tell Ma-Ma bye-bye. All right, good night all."

As an adult, "the wall" allowed me to repel the yelling and negative comments and continue to love my mom, visit with her, ensure she had a relationship with my kids, and throw great events with her. I even told my sister she should ignore the negativity, be the bigger person and just deal with it (like me—remember, I'm the good person).

The wall did not work this time. I was angry, and it just would not leave me. I couldn't accept this intentional pain inflicted on me. Maybe the wall was Little Kendra; she had dealt with so much that she protected me from my pain and allowed me to compartmentalize (put my hurt feelings in a box) and keep it moving. Why did Little Kendra take the wall when she got healed? Why did she refuse to come back so I could feel better about my mom and this incident? Why did she force Big Kendra to have to deal with this? I had to confront this, so I called her.

"Hi Mom. We need to talk. Can you meet me tomorrow at Panera at six p.m.?"

"Okay," she answered.

"Okay. Thanks. See you then." She agreed. I did it. I had to get this out. It needed to be in a public place where it wouldn't get too loud or disrespectful. No one else from the family needed to be there. Just me and her.

It was two minutes after six; I was waiting at Panera looking out the window. She pulled up. I felt the butterflies in my stomach. I had rehearsed this in my head, but I was going to speak from the heart. She walked in with the angry face.

"Hi Mom."

"Hi," she said. She went to order some food and came back with a turkey sandwich. She took two bites, and I began. I started off talking about yelling at the cookout.

"I will yell at you!" my mom said.

"No, you will not," I replied. "I am a grown woman and won't take that anymore."

She backed down, sat back, and continued our conversation. (I understand now this is why Little Kendra left me. She would have never had the strength to confront my mom like this and be willing to accept the consequences.) Innately, I knew my mom felt the difference too; that's why she became silent at my boldness. (I like this Big Kendra!)

My overwhelming theme for the conversation was that I never felt unconditional love from my mother. The love from my dad and paternal grandmother could not replace that. She did not realize I'd always longed for her unconditional love; she thought I was satisfied with just my dad's side of the family supporting me. I will always honor, love, and appreciate my paternal grandmother, but nothing could take the place of my mother, the one who carried me, and the one who was supposed to love me no matter what. Like the mothers my friends have who love them. I understood why my clients who were foster kids always longed for their mothers. I did too.

I knew my mom had the capacity to love unconditionally. My mom was a sacrificial lover; she would unselfishly give of herself to the end if she loved you. (I think that is where I got my strong sense of loyalty and friendship.) She loved her mom and visited her almost every day. She knew all the terminology about her lung disease, the oxygen tank, and all the precautions that needed to be taken.

Speaking of my maternal grandmother, she displayed unconditional love too. She loved my uncles through all their misdeeds. They always knew their mom did not approve of their bad choices, but she loved them, cared for them, and they could always come to her for support, no matter what. My mom followed her mother's example and loved her brothers too. (It seemed my mom allowed her brothers and friends to be imperfect, but not me. I had to be perfect. I had never been addicted to drugs or spent a day in jail, had become a successful lawyer and community servant, but always felt if I said the wrong thing, my mom's pride, support, and love would wane.)

"Mom, I know you have the capacity to love unconditionally. You loved your mom. Your mom loved you. You even loved my sister unconditionally, just not me." I said it.

"Don't you think I know that, Kendra?" Her face turned pink, her eyes welled up, and tears flowed down her cheeks. "I know what I did. I regret it every day!" She kept crying and speaking through her tears. "I didn't realize you wanted me. I thought your grandmother was enough for you!" (I smiled a little, on the inside; maybe she did always care.)

"No, Mom, I always wanted unconditional love from my mother. I always needed you."

We were both in tears, ended with a long hug, and said we loved each other. I felt good about this life-changing talk. (I did it!!) We parted ways; my mom never finished her turkey sandwich.

Conclusion

Thank you for sharing in my healing process. I hope that you were able to relate to some aspect of experiencing hurt but recognize you should always have hope because as Luke 1:37 tells us "For with God, nothing shall be impossible." It is possible for God to heal the relationship between mothers and daughters, fathers and sons, friends, co-workers, church members and any others.

Once I was healed, it is like the world got brighter, my load was lighter, and I felt a freedom and happiness I never felt before. I was free to fully forgive (I thought I had done it over the years, but I had not) and free to discuss my prior pain. I had many close friends who, upon learning of my childhood traumas, said, "I never would have known" or "You never told me you were dealing with all of that!" They didn't know because I was able to compartmentalize my pain, put it to the side and keep moving on with my education, career, marriage, family, divorce, etc. I'm sure there are plenty of professional women still in mental bondage as I was. BUT GOD!! Through it all, God never left me. He comforted me and carried me until I was able to stand on my own, face my pain, release it, and receive the inner peace and joy that surpasses all understanding. I see that He chose me many years ago for such a time as this. The prophecy that was spoken over me many years ago that I would "be able to heal the hearts of women through the Word of God" has become a way of life for me. My willingness to share just pieces of my story has given permission and freedom to many other women to face their pain and heal the girls within them. TO GOD BE THE GLORY!!!

2 Corinthians 4:16-18

Therefore we do not lose heart. Though outwardly we are wasting away, yet inwardly we are being renewed day by day. For our light and momentary troubles are achieving for us an eternal glory that far outweighs them all. So we fix our eyes not on what is seen, but on what is unseen, since what is seen is temporary, but what is unseen is eternal.

 **Sandra Chaney**, Compelling Change Agent, Nonprofit Strategist and Grant Specialist, Bestselling Author, Coach and National Speaker, is on a global assignment to help women live and love beyond their titles, be more than their businesses/ ministries and to transform their lives to manifest the mission they were created to bring forth. The wind beneath her wings is from the loving and faithful support of her husband Kevin Chaney and the pulse of her heart, Maurice Dews, her son. Sandra lives her life by this motto: "Everything I do, say and offer the world will come from a deep place of love!" To learn more about Sandra visit www.sandrachaney.com.

Time to Tell the Truth
By Sandra Chaney

The Lie

Will the real Sandra Chaney please stand up? Do you remember the show "To Tell the Truth?" In this show three people were introduced, all claiming to be the actual person. Each person was asked his or her name. They all gave the same name, pretending to be someone else. In this game, a group of panelists was given permission to ask questions of each challenger. The real person had sworn to give truthful answers and the imposters were allowed to lie. They pretended to be the actual character. Well "to tell the truth," I struggled with knowing who I was. I gave myself permission to lie about my past and pretend to be someone I was not. In other words, I allowed other people's opinions, ideas, suggestions and thoughts to shape me. I looked for the real me, as the cliché states, in all the wrong places. When asked to really talk about me authentically, it was always difficult. I always started out with what I did, not who I was. This quest to find out who the real me was was about to come to a head.

Fear kept me in a trapped place. Even though I was accomplished (had a great job, drove a nice car, owned my own home), I still was in hiding. Fear had me: 1) trying to please others, 2) over-analyzing everything, 3) putting everyone and everything before me and 4) not fulfilling my true purpose. Fear had me thinking my life was not worth anything and that everyone would be better off without me. So I attempted suicide. Will the REAL Sandra Mizell Chaney stand up? Fear kept me stuck in victimhood and the woe-is-me syndrome. Although I had overcome domestic violence, homelessness, sexual assault, jail and single parenting, I still saw myself as not being worthy. The truth of the matter was fear had me living a lie. Even though those things happened to me, they were not me. If only I could believe. After a while that lie was depleting my cup and now, I was giving from an empty cup.

Acknowledging the truth

For a long time, I was giving from an empty cup and did not even realize it. I pretended to be this strong, loving, corporate; had-it-all-together woman, when all the while I was living a life of rejection, depression, and loneliness with a heart full of secrets and shame. *I failed at my first marriage,* I told myself. *Now I am a single mom raising a boy and I don't know what I'm doing. So, this makes me a bad mother,* I kept thinking. *I don't have any friends because no one understands my pain and the abuse I suffered,* so I thought. You know what, it was easier to bury these negative feelings and pretend they didn't exist than it was to feel and deal. What I did was put up a wall. I only allowed people to come just so far into my world. I was afraid they would see the real me and I would be rejected all over again. This is where the acknowledgement comes in. Nothing will change until you can be truthful with yourself. I would see other women who had it all together and wanted to be them, but at the same time I hated them and felt intimidated by them. Why? I did not know who I was, and my cup was depleted. I heard someone say, "When you have not truly healed the wounds of your past, forgiven self and others, you will continue to bleed into your destiny." I was bleeding and it was time for a change.

Attempting suicide was my cry for help. I did not know how to ask for help. It was easier to pretend. The suicide attempt forced me to start dealing with me. My cup was completely empty. God sent me several lifelines; however, my ego (the flesh) was louder than the voice of God. Looking at my own stuff was not always easy, but necessary to fulfilling my purpose and destiny. It meant facing some pains, wounds and rejections that I had buried. I dealt with feelings of an abusive marriage, death of that marriage, homelessness, single parenting, job loss, financial loss, and family hurt (mother and father). I had to stop and acknowledge my truths and stop the bleeding. The truth was I allowed fear to keep re-living my story. It was time to tell myself the truth, so the true healing could begin.

A new life begins

Will the real Sandra Chaney stand up? Facing and acknowledging the truth was a process. Getting naked and facing self was a choice I decided to make. Well, since we are telling the truth, I was forced to deal with me when I attempted suicide. When I was found, I was taken to the emergency room by someone I least expected. God will use the very people you think are attempting to hurt you to help you. Anyhow, when I arrived at the emergency room, they decided to keep me and put me on suicide watch. That meant I was not going home for a minute. I ended up staying in a residential home with beautiful landscaping, deer roaming and other amenities. When God is in control, He is going to do it his way. It was certainly a strange place for me to be. My son was staying with his father's side of the family. My job gave me the time I needed. So I had no excuse. They were all removed. Again, God was and still is in control of my life.

The choice was now up to me to take advantage of the blessing that was right in front of me, yet I still struggled with facing the hurt and pain I had buried so deep. Getting naked is not easy; however, it was necessary if I expected to heal these wounds. New life begins where the pain first started. For me facing the pain meant facing the lie to get to the truth. The fact of the matter was those things I listed earlier happened to me; they were not me. Those things that happened came to teach me some things. It was up to me to learn the lesson. In the lesson, forgiveness was important. Forgiving me was paramount and part of my healing process. In order to forgive myself, I had to share my story with myself, through journaling and counseling. Let me say this: I had to recognize that this was not an overnight process. There were times I wanted to give up because it seemed easier to mask and pretend that all was well. I thought if I could just get back to my corporate job, my fancy cute clothes and my life, I could handle this. Well, doing that only meant it was a matter of time before I truly crashed and burned. So I reminded myself to take advantage of this new life I was given and the gift I was handed. What I discovered is that while I was shedding, it did not always feel good, but I could choose how I wanted to be in the process. During this process, I cried a lot, cursed, shut down, screamed, laughed, and danced in private, in counseling and in group support. I did what I needed to do to heal and release myself from all that weight I was carrying.

One thing I became aware of was what my son was going through because of my stuff. There is so much I could say here. I will say this: I needed to deal with the feeling of not being a good mother. This took me a while because I had to first deal with the fact that I got pregnant just to have someone who loved me unconditionally. When I got pregnant, I did not understand what being a mother meant. I didn't have a good relationship with my mother. I really did not know what I was getting myself into. I felt like I was failing, and it caused me to not want to be a mother. Hence, I thought I was not worthy and that everyone would be better off if I was not here. I know this may seem harsh, but it was my truth and I had to face it if I was going to really heal and if my son was going to heal. I could pick and choose what I really wanted to heal, but then I would not serve the gift of a new life I had been given.

Like I said, this is a process. So some years later and during a 40-day surrender fast, I came face to face with how much "stuff" I had been carrying and what it was doing to me. While I had done a lot of work, I was still hiding and dealing with the fear of rejection and unworthiness. I once again felt like I had failed. The difference this time was I had mentors in my life. I remember one of them saying to me, "Rome was not built in a day. Celebrate the work you've done and stop beating yourself up." Through the fast I committed to going deeper and releasing what no longer served me. I faced my truths as I had in the past, even when they were painful. What I found interesting was that at every elevation in my life, I had to release what no longer served me. So, I stopped resisting and ignoring things when they were revealed in my life. I stopped pretending they did not exist. I am still hard-headed from time to time. God will always send a ram in the bush to knock me upside my head.

There is a Sam Cooke song titled "A change is Gonna Come." He states in the song, "I was born in a little tent and just like the river I've been running ever since." I had to face the tents (shame, feeling unloved, not loving self, insecurities, feelings of rejection) that would show up when I least expected. I journaled or talked out whatever came up with my mentors or close circle, so that I could release. I was ready for my true authentic self to finally emerge. To keep her from hiding, I shared my truth with others.

In my secret place, I learned to start where the pain first began. While it was not easy to truly see me, I was ready for a change. I allowed myself to feel what I had been hiding. That was so painful, and it hurt. I cried so much, but it was necessary in order to be free. I then forgave myself for self-sabotaging and playing the blame game. I also forgave others, realizing that I might never hear an apology from them. It was okay, because I was choosing to love me, love unconditionally and live my best life. God's greatest commandment is to love. Even though I heard it a million times (okay, maybe not that many times), I finally learned it for myself.

While fear attempts to pop up every now and again, I do not allow it to stop me in my tracks. I tell myself the truth about what I am feeling. When I feel rejection creeping up, I do share love with someone else – sometimes with the person I am feeling rejected by. Usually when I am feeling rejected it has nothing to do with the other person. So I get quiet and go within to understand what this feeling is all about. God and I have deep conversations in the car, at the beach, in the bathtub and in nature. This is how I handle every negative feeling that attempts to come up. In my quiet time I reframe my words and thoughts because I can. God reminds me daily that I have the power. One of my favorite scriptures is Proverbs 3:5-6: "Trust God with all your heart and lean not to your own understanding; In all your ways acknowledge Him and He shall direct your path." When I did not understand what to do, I read this scripture. When I was scared, I read this scripture. When I needed direction, I read this scripture. Believe me, there were times when I couldn't or didn't want to recall any scriptures. Yet God was the one constant in my life because I AM that I AM. He is me and I am him.

Today my life is WAY better. God is so amazing! He opened doors for me to share my life with others. I've had the honor of traveling around the country helping faith-based organizations create ministries/programs to help the women in their communities heal from domestic violence. My name was submitted to be on a panel for a federal government conference with doctors to talk about substance abuse, domestic violence and mental health. It was a scary yet amazing experience. Because of my background and experience, I've facilitated numerous retreats as a speaker on healing, helped women create nonprofits (I am an Expert Nonprofit and Grant Strategist), helped others get funding for their non-profits, assisted people with completing their books and coached people to their next levels using my life experiences (both personal and business). In addition, I became a bestselling author of four books and an author of seven so far. I'm just getting started. I live my life by this motto: Everything I do, say and offer the world comes from a deep place of love. I'm still doing my work because I still have my moments of self-doubt, rejection and unworthiness. In those moments, I remind myself that I am a spiritual being having a human experience and it's okay. I put the ego (the human side) in time-out so that the spiritual me can rise. I remember who I am. I look at myself in the mirror and speak over myself. I am who I say I am!

It was time "to tell the truth" and I am glad I did. A serious weight has been lifted and I feel very liberated. I challenge you to come face to face with who you are. Do you still have hurt, pain, unforgiveness, bitterness, shame, etc. in your heart? It's time to be free, so that you can fully be the expression of love you were created to be. You were created to be great! Your gifts, dreams and visions are waiting to be unleashed! It's time to stop living the lie! It's time "To Tell the Truth!"

Kelly Bouchard is an international success coach, empowerment speaker and trainer.

She is President of Bouchard International, a company dedicated to helping people create massive success.

She successfully launched and managed a cosmetic company that achieved multi-million-dollar success, developing thousands of entrepreneurial consultants nationwide. The business was then purchased by multinational Tupperware and Kelly went on to found Bouchard International.

Kelly is thrilled to share her learned experience with today's entrepreneurs, helping them surpass their wildest expectations.

You Can Blame, or You Can Bloom

By Kelly Bouchard

Choose to Bloom

"Every generation blames the one before." -Mike and the Mechanics

There is so much power in that statement. There's a lot of truth to it and there's also a choice we can make to stop the blame, learn from it and recreate something positive for the next generation.

From the outside, our home looked like your typical middle-class happy family home: both parents working, three children, two cars and every once in a while, a dog. We went on vacations and if I look through old pictures, I see a few birthday parties.

I guess you could say my parents did the best they could, considering their upbringing. I think Dad's family was okay because we loved our grandparents, but I suspect something bad happened to my father because he drank a lot and although he had a sense of humor, he had an awful lot of anger. When you combine rage and alcohol it can get really ugly. My brother and sister suffered his wrath a lot more than I did because I was much younger and smaller than they were, so I don't think my father could bring himself to hit me the same way he hit them.

Mom's upbringing was anything but normal. Her dad was an absolute loser and her mom was not a very loving person. My aunt tells me that he would beat them senselessly and often times they'd get evicted from where they lived and more times than not, they had nothing to eat.

So when you consider my parents' home life, anything better than that would seem great. Unfortunately, it wasn't.

You can put a roof over anyone's head and feed them three meals a day, but it doesn't mean you can drink and fight and create a chaotic environment leading to total dysfunction and call that a happy family.

That's what we had. Chaos and dysfunction on the inside, picture postcard perfect on the outside.

Being the youngest in the family, I sort of fell through the cracks. My parents both worked 12-hour days, including a long commute. My brother and sister went to high school, so I was a latch-key kid. I came home to an empty house every single day. Years later my brother left for college and my sister ran away. So again, I found myself alone. I had a lot of friends, but my parents didn't have time for me. That was when I started to really get into trouble. There's nothing worse than feeling like you don't matter. I started smoking cigarettes as my first sign of rebellion, but my parents were oblivious to it because they were so involved in their own drama. I started drinking when I was 11, the summer before going into high school. Where I grew up, high school started in grade 7 and ended in grade 11. As soon as I got to high school, I got right into smoking weed, cutting class and just getting downright wasted. All I ever wanted to do was get high.

I convinced my dad to let me quit school when I was in ninth grade because I wasn't learning anything. He told me I could quit if I found a job. I guess he thought nobody would hire me, but I found one and then another and another. I worked at a few restaurants and really didn't like it, but it gave me money to party with and I did that a lot. My parents started getting on my case and there was a lot of other stuff going on in our family, so I decided to run away. Because my sister had run away years earlier and ended up in the court system, my parents made it abundantly clear to me that they wouldn't come chasing after me. They told me if I wanted to leave, to go ahead. More reinforcement to how little I mattered. That's when I decided to go full out and get as drunk and high as I could every day. It's pretty much a big blur, but I ended up in the worst places.

The bar down the street from our house was a biker bar and I was in there all the time. All my friends were much older than I was so I was always somewhere I shouldn't be. My drug habit was starting to get costly, so I thought I'd follow in the footsteps of my mother and get myself an office job. I had little education, I looked a lot younger than I was because I was so tiny, yet I believe my enthusiasm to want to do a great job and make something out of my life always convinced people to give me a chance. I finally got a great job in a pharmaceutical company. It was amazing and I was making great money. Great money meant great partying. From there my life just spiraled downward. My drug use was way out of control. There was a whole different drama going on in our family and I just couldn't see life getting any better. The Bible says, "Without a vision, my people perish." I did. I just didn't want to live anymore. Everyone around me had problems. My home life was bad, the people I hung out with were all into drugs, either selling or doing them. There were gang members, some dying, some going to jail. It wasn't uncommon to see some of my friends headline the newspapers for a most recent drug bust or even getting shot and killed. I remember once when my mom was talking about a guy who'd been killed while trying to rob someone, I thought, *Wow, if she only knew I had just had a beer and shot a couple of games of pool with him days earlier.* Some of my friends had their kids taken away from them; even the dealers were losing property because they were getting high on their own supply. It was just a big mess and I wanted out. I tried to end my life. I attempted suicide four times. It wasn't just a cry for help as most doctors would say; it was a real cry of "get me out of here; I have nothing to live for."

Then God gave me something to live for. He gave me someone. He gave me my firstborn son, my beautiful baby boy, Kenny! That was the turning point in my life. Yes, I was an unwed teenage mom but that was okay, I had a purpose now and I was determined to make it. This was my chance at changing the course of the past generations of our family. I gave everything up cold turkey. No smoking, no drinking, no drugs. Look at God! I wanted my baby to be healthy and have a chance at life. Mike, Kenny's dad, wasn't quite ready for this lifestyle change. He suffered from PTSD and had been on drugs for so many years, he wasn't remotely close to quitting anytime soon.

I moved back in with my parents during my pregnancy. You might as well say I went to jail, because they had me under surveillance at all times. I was being punished for the mess I had made of my life. I mean after all, what would the neighbors say?

I'll always remember the day Kenny was born and holding him for the very first time. It was instant love. I remember looking at him and promising him a good life. I promised that we were going to make it and that he was going to come before anyone or anything. He mattered and I wanted him to know this and to feel loved and cared for.

I was doing all right for a while but every time my friends would call or come around, they would make sure to tell me about all the fun they were having and how much I was missing out. If they stopped by, they'd be looking great and showing me their latest fashion; meanwhile, I didn't have two pennies to rub together. Any money I had went to taking care of Kenny. I stayed in for a long time and then finally one night I went out. There were a few people who were happy to see me back, not because they missed me, but because they were hoping I'd fall flat on my face and get back to that party life. Sadly, I did slip up a couple of times. I was just a kid myself. Then came another turning point; it was the step before rock bottom. I was out with a good friend. We'd been drinking, and she was shooting coke. She asked me if I wanted to do it too. I had sniffed a lot of coke in my drug days, but I had never shot it and I was kind of proud that I hadn't. I saw the destruction of everyone around me. Unfortunately, this time I gave in. I did it a couple of times afterward. I came home once after a night of shooting coke and looked at my son and asked myself how I could do this to him. How could I be such a loser? I had promised him a good life! He was innocent and depending on me. It wasn't too late though. I could still keep that promise. The volatility at my parents' home had reached a climax where it became unbearable and that's when I decided to go find a place to stay.

I lived on my own for a bit. It was hard though. There were days where I couldn't even afford Kool-Aid if I wanted to buy baby food. I ended up homeless in a shelter. No hope, no plans, no options. That was my rock bottom. Here I was, in a shelter for abused women with my son, the one I promised a good life. That was it, I'd had enough! I decided I was going to get a good job, I had done that before. I was going to move out of the crazy neighborhood I was in and just start all over again, and I did. Mike and I got back together; he was trying hard to get straight. I got pregnant again and that was Mike's turning point.

He stopped everything, cleaned up his life and went back to get a corporate job.

Along came our newest gift from God, our son Christopher. I remember when they put Chris in my arms, I looked at him and I was in awe at how much God had blessed us once again. I was so in love with this cute little bundle of joy and I thanked him for making us a family now. It was much easier to make good on our promise this time. Kenny had been my turning point and Chris was now Mike's turning point.

To whom much is given, much is required. We slowly built our way up. Mike and I got married. We never drank or did drugs again. I chose to stay home with my boys because I had felt so unloved and unwanted growing up that I didn't want my children to feel that pain. I am not saying that going to work outside the home causes that, but that was my reality. Mike got a really great job and built a great career. We started going to church with Mike's mom every Sunday and then we'd go to her house for breakfast. It was the beginning of new family traditions.

God was blessing us exceedingly and abundantly more than we could ask or imagine. We bought our first home and there our daughter Tamara was born. Miracle number three: I forgot to mention earlier that Mike was told he couldn't have children. When the nurse put Tamara in my arms, I was in heaven. She was beautiful and she was confirmation that we were moving in the direction of our dreams. With each new baby came more and more blessings. Mike moved quickly in business to make up for lost time. Joel 2:25 says, "The Lord will restore the years that the locusts have taken." He certainly did!

As the kids grew and my youngest went to school, we decided to start our own company. That way I could create my own career and still be there for my kids. We partnered with a Dallas-based cosmetics company, owning the Canadian subsidiary. I loved it!

We were now in a position of helping women across Canada build their businesses while enjoying their family time and living the lives of their dreams. I loved watching women achieve what they once thought impossible. Our company became a multi-million-dollar success.

After the company was sold to Tupperware, I chose to continue the path of helping women succeed in life and in business. I dedicated myself to learning everything I possibly could about human potential, personal development and success in business. I made sure to learn from the very best. I studied under Jack Canfield and had the opportunity to work closely with him, staffing his events. Les Brown, arguably one of the best motivational speakers, was my mentor. I traveled with him to many events and shared the stage with him numerous times. As I worked to hone my speaking skills, I noticed many speakers quoting scripture from the Bible. Although I always believed in God and prayed to Him during my darkest days, I had never opened a Bible in my life. I now had to open a Bible to see what these quotes were all about. Isn't it amazing how God will meet you where you are? This deepened my relationship with God and I learned how loved I was, how I mattered and how God had a purpose and plan for my life. He has one for you too. He brought me close and showed me that He was there during my pain and that he heard my every prayer and that I was forgiven. Now it was time for me to help heal others, to inspire and lead and help them see their vision...the one God has for them.

I went from being a high school dropout, a runaway, a suicidal messed-up teen and a drug addict, to becoming a mom, a wife, a business owner, a motivational speaker and success coach making a positive difference in the lives of many. I have the privilege of speaking in schools to help teens build their confidence and self-esteem. In addition, I offer programs and have helped young women in maximum security prisons regain hope for a brighter future.

I help women get clear on their purpose, gain the confidence to pursue it with absolute certainty and stay fully committed until they see it materialize with great success!

As for my family, I am more than happy to say I broke that generational curse. My children are all grown now and lead happy lives. They know how much Mike and I love and adore them. My dream was to have a tight, loving family where kids knew they mattered, that they were special and created to live and love greatly. When we're all together, it's the greatest feeling in the world. And yes, we've had ups and downs but one thing we know for sure, we've all got each other.

As I type this, I am sitting in my condo in Honolulu, Hawaii where I've lived for the last six years. I have the most spectacular ocean view of Waikiki Beach and to the left of me, I can see Diamond Head mountain. I don't say this to brag. I say this to let you know that if God can do this for me, He will definitely do what He's planned and promised for you. His Word clearly states He has no favorites...only Great Favor.

To God be all the Glory.

• •

Romans 8:31

What, then, shall we say in

response to these things?

If God is for us, who can be

against us?

• •

Gladys Peaches Kenney is a Licensed Social Worker, Faith Motivating Coach, Author, Speaker and Cancer Survivor.

She graduated from the University of Maryland at Baltimore School of Social Work, earning her Master's degree. With over 20 years of experience, she has unselfishly provided outreach and direct services to the community. Her faith in God is her driving force, which compels her to help coach and serve others.

She has been featured on radio stations and in magazines sharing her amazing journey of conquering cancer with a smile. She wrote about her battle with breast cancer in her first book, *Stepping Out on Faith, Dare to Dream: A Journal of Faith & Workbook*. Astonishingly, it was published within 48 hours of her first surgery to remove breast cancer, with the Workbook completed 30 days later. In addition, her third book, *iRise: Stories of Triumph*, which she co-authored, was published in January 2019. Finally, the last two jobs/contracts she received, she never applied for, but the organizations called her in for an interview and hired her immediately, thus demonstrating walking by FAITH is her Lifestyle.

For Bookings Contact: www.faithsteps8.com
Email: faithsteps8@gmail.com
Facebook @SteppingOutonFaithDaretoDream
Instagram @Faithsteps8

Broken Silence: Unmuted & Speaking Out with a Purpose

By Gladys Peaches Kenney

I Won't be Silenced

This story is dedicated to those of you who did not have the courage to tell your story but wanted to. This is for the person who felt like nobody needed to hear their words and you buried your desires of reaching higher. Before you finish reading this chapter, you will grab your keys and you will rise from being silent like I was, un-muted and unstoppable. Today is the beginning of you unleashing what the devil tried to hide because he knew that God was going to use your voice one day. If you think you cannot do it, think again. I will give you reasons why it is vital for you and me to stop being Silent. Speak Loud, Speak Up, Speak Proud.

Broken, according to Google, means:

verb
    1. past participle of break.
adjective
    1. having been fractured or damaged and no longer in one
       piece or in working order. "a broken arm"

synonyms: smashed, shattered, fragmented, splintered, crushed, snapped

2. (of a person) having given up all hope; despairing. "he went to his grave a broken man" synonyms: defeated, beaten, subdued

Broken Silence is the untold version of one's truth. The irony of the word broken is that it is normally viewed in a negative context. Look at the synonyms for the word broken: beaten, defeated and subdued. If someone is subdued and defeated, they have lost the battle. Take the word silent, which means that one is quiet, without words or noise. Yet combining two forms of the words "broken silence," you are declaring that the quiet and wordlessness are over, because they have been defeated and subdued. Your words will now be heard and not lost.

Can you just picture someone taking their hand to cover up your mouth or putting tape over your lips just as your brain has directed your mouth to formulate a thought, then that thought is trapped in mid-sentence? That is what it is like to be on mute: you have something meaningful to speak but fear, intimidation, and judgment have blocked you. You are left silent. Often, I was silent more than I ever wanted due to being scared. After you attempt to speak, and you are directed not to talk, then you learn the practice of holding it in.

Imagine hearing negative words daily as a child and you grow up into adulthood experiencing toxic words as well. It's no wonder I remained on mute for so long. This is likely a shocker to those who know me now because I was normally either quiet or smiling so often that it was overlooked. There was some popularity that I had on the surface. I was the life of the party in my adult years, but my feelings were sometimes masked. Sometimes I laughed to prevent myself from crying or being angry and frustrated.

"Be quiet!" "Shut Up!" "Hush up, 'cause nobody wants to hear that." "That's dumb and stupid!" "You may look smart, but you don't have any common sense." "You are too black and ugly." "Kids are meant to be seen not heard" and "kids should stay out of grown folks' business." The power of words can elevate your existence or send you a fast ticket to your emotional death. With emotional death, you are physically alive but your drive to fulfill your passions is faint.

Too many times after hearing negative words, it was like a noose being wrapped around my neck, killing inner dreams of confidence. There were parts of my childhood and adulthood which had me afraid to speak out, to speak my truth.

The truth is, I didn't feel comfortable revealing my honest opinions due to fear of rejection and fear of losing friendships. Sometimes the people I was holding on to were not really my friends at all. I would allow people with strong personalities to take advantage of me because I did not have the stamina. There was little backbone in me at all. I admired people who spoke their mind and did not care about what others thought. I was fascinated by their courage, but sometimes angry that they did not spare the feelings of the person they spoke about. Being a sensitive person and realizing how fragile my heart was, it was often difficult for me to say mean things to people even when they made me upset. I would try to be considerate of their feelings. Yes, I would cross those lines, but I tried not to. I had to rehearse what I would say if I wanted to say something negative back to someone who offended or picked on me. Anger would fill me, but I would take it out on myself, questioning why I did not think of something witty to say as a rebuttal, and why I allowed folks to mistreat me with their words and actions. Being nice and pleasant did not seem to serve me well socially because it was viewed as a sign of weakness. I wanted to be bold like my big sister who could talk stuff and back it up. Fighting was always a last resort for me.

I was a slave to others' opinions of me, because I wanted to be liked by everyone. I know that everyone is not destined to be your friend, but I was longing to feel accepted and a part of something. When there is a void and you do not walk in confidence, then insecurities manifest.

Time Capsule

I recall in school how there were classmates who had most of the students afraid of them because of their demeanor and height. The school bullies were about a year or two older than the rest of us. In my mind, I would stick up for myself and others to tell them leave us alone and pick on someone their own size. However, I would shrink into my inner shell and not utter a word unless I mumbled to prevent being heard. The fear of having to defend my opinion verbally and physically kept me in "check" since I always wanted things to be peaceful and "perfect." Arguing was not my strength and with little practice, it did not make sense to bring attention to that area.

On the other hand, I had a girl that I grew up with—we were friends, but we would have fights sometimes too. She was more vocal and wilder than I was. I was afraid of her sometimes because she spoke with boldness and conviction like she would really do whatever she said. Many times, I tried to avoid fighting because I'd rather we'd get along, even though I did not like the way she and others would pick on and tease me. She and others thought it was funny, but inside I would feel very embarrassed and angry that I was not as brave. One time during our disagreements and fights, I ran home crying after she bit me. At that moment, it seemed like time stopped as I saw blood streaming down my hand. As I was screaming to my dad that my friend beat me up, he screamed at me and told me that I better go kick her #%}%^*! or he was going to beat mine for not fighting back to defend myself. My dad knew our history of being friends, then fighting, all initiated by her. I was not the type to bother anybody, so he knew I was being taken advantage of. In order to obey my dad, defend my honor and prevent a butt whipping, I went back to fight my friend but bit her back. After I beat her up this time and stood up for myself, we never came to that point again. I had proven myself that time. However, fear kept me from continuing to walk in that boldness.

Fear not

Fear is a dominating force that will either prompt you into action or freeze you into a statue. Most often, I was frozen to move past my fears of speaking out with my opinions. It was decades later when I discovered that fear was false evidence appearing real. God tells us to fear not several times throughout the Bible.

No Limits, no boundaries

I did not know that I could let others know my preferences and things that I liked but more so what I did not like. My experience had been when people shared what they did not like, it was spoken in such a negative tone of disgust and anger that I did not want to be associated with that. I was dealing with pride and protecting my reputation and image. I wanted a positive one and to me, with my limited thinking, I thought that telling others what you did not like was like complaining or being ungrateful. Again, it was my experience of hearing people's explicit language and angry tone when they said they did not care about a particular person, place, or thing.

However, I know today sharing your likes and dislikes is important, but it needs to be delivered tactfully. Disclaimer:

Please note if you are threatened or your safety or that of those close to you is at risk then being tactful is not important at that point. Establishing your safety is what makes sense. Speak with boldness that you need that person to respect you and yours with authority.

I think I figured out that I was focusing on the "Lamb of God" and forgetting about the "Lion of Judah." Jesus was very humble and peaceful, but he also overturned the tables when he witnessed the injustice of the people in the temple. Now, I'm finally speaking up for myself. People thought I was crazy for so long because I let people get over on me.

Three years ago, when I was just getting started, I was talking to this guy who told me, "Dag, you talk too much." The enemy attempted to have me to dim my light and stop speaking again. At first, I had a comeback, but after he spoke it more than twice, I gradually started to believe that lie. I noticed I wasn't as hyped as I normally was about God and life when I was communicating with him. Then after seeing more, that he was another Ishmael, God said He wasn't the one and I stopped talking to him. Once I did that, my book was published. He was a stumbling block that was trying to get me off my game. Again, the devil was trying to use a relationship to hinder my purpose and keep me from speaking out. I must shine. I don't have any animosity toward him; he just wasn't for me. It gave me much joy to recently share with him how God has been using me. I told him that all my talking is finally paying off.

How did this peeping turtle rise tall like a giraffe and shift my crown of glory as the Queen that I am discovering daily? I can tell you it did not happen overnight at all but looking back, I must attribute my beginning boldness to my Lord and Savior Jesus Christ. I rededicated and submitted my life to Christ in the late 90s after losing a loved one.

Life Changing

Rededicating my heart and life to God was the pivotal decision that led to the "tape" coming off my mouth. The supernatural boldness that I felt in God was amazing to me. Now I learned some scriptures like Philippians 4:13, that I could do all things through Christ Jesus. Another scripture was that God had plans for me of hope and not failure and an expected end, in Jeremiah 29:11. Three of my favorite ones are, for me to basically put God first and then He will add to me what I need, which is found in Matthew 6:33; no weapon formed against me will be able to flourish, found at Isaiah 54:17; and if I make a mistake I can tell God and He will forgive me and cleanse me, I John 1:9. Although I paraphrased the scriptures above, memorizing those scriptures was helpful, but living these scriptures made it real. For example, when I am and was faced with challenges I would pray and quote those words in the scripture. Trust me, many challenges happened.

Catapult

Now that I've stepped out of the old me to what God has for me, I'm moving forward, not worrying what they say or think. I'm hearing what God is saying and stepping out of the box, going deeper in the waters.

Now it is making sense; the pieces of the puzzle are formulated. The enemy of my soul wanted me to stay on mute because he realized once I spoke what God said, then people would be different and transformed. Their lives would be impacted and filled with joy and love. Today I am a Motivational Speaker who will soon be an international speaker. God spoke that he was taking me to the nations as recently as July 2017 in the ocean of Fort Lauderdale. I am passport-ready to share my story.

Impactful

Making a difference and impact to those near and far is how I will continue to live my life. Tears of joy almost rolled from my eyes after I was able to do presentations on my new job for the parents at the school. The workshops that I have been teaching are to build their self-esteem, to inspire and motivate them to Dream Bigger. In a very short time, just a few weeks to be more exact, I have witnessed very shy, quiet, and withdrawn women gradually come out of their hidden places and reconnect with other parents who they normally passed by in the school hallways. These parents have been volunteering their services and after one of the workshops, they were taught the importance and benefits of volunteering and serving others. The transformation that I am already beginning to witness again almost makes me cry. When a few of the parents were asked on the spot how I had impacted their lives in the past five weeks, they collectively agreed that I was there to help and connect with the school; I was pushing them to be their best; and I was their voice that they thought was lost long ago. After those profound words, I told the parents, "This is why I do what I do." I can relate so much to that longing to be heard and noticed by others for something positive. I am fulfilling my God-given assignment.

Won't He Do It?

This is dedicated to pure praise and glory to my Heavenly Father for the great things He has Done. #CanIJustTellYouWhatGodDid? is an expression that I began using heavily within the past two and a half years, after experiencing two major blows that tend to take many folks out. However, God has blessed me to overcome so many tragedies, it undoubtedly boosted my Faith, and I love to share it to increase others. I declare that I am Set Apart and Chosen.

I knew that I was Set Apart and Chosen when God ordered my steps to meet people who had the answer to my problems. When I'd take a different route than normal and run into someone that God placed on my heart earlier in the week. When I would see that person and be able to encourage and pray with them and let them know that God had them on His heart.

I knew I was Set Apart and Chosen because I was able to lose my employment and be more at peace and able to do more with less. I definitely know that God's hands are over me, because after giving my testimony of celibacy, that I was waiting on God's Best because I tried to date my way and it did not work, a guy told me that it seemed like God had just put me in a jar to preserve me on the shelf until I got the right one. That gave me a revelation of why I had been single for so long. It has encouraged me for years. Last, I know that I am Set Apart and Chosen because as a #FaithMotivator and #FaithCoach I push people to pursue their dreams by Faith and Works despite the challenges they are experiencing. For example, I had someone old enough to be my mother telling they needed me to impart some of what is within me into them because they had been listening to what I say. She said that I motivated her, and she wanted me to be her mentor.

Experiencing the Glimpse

As the year 2018 came to a close, writing this fourth book provided such a revelation of my purpose. It allowed my ideas and dreams to burst from within but now outward. It was breaking off past chains that I created and allowed others to put on me. The freedoms of knowing who you are and who you belong to are powerful tools that unlock many doors. Not being afraid anymore... Being free from people and things that could harm or try to control me. I am Free. I am God's Chosen. I have been

Set Apart for such a time as this. The creativity that flows in my mind does not seem to be able to allow me to type as fast as I want to share with you. You must grab hold of the fact that the devil does come to steal, kill, and destroy your life. Therefore, he will entice you to take detours that are not part of God's original plan for your life in hopes that you are too distracted to ever return to Jesus to receive your reward and crown. The enemy lies and tells you that you cannot make it because of your rough childhood, broken marriage and your lack of education. Yet the God that we serve looks beyond all of that and He can make our crooked ways straight. Grab hold of what you know or believe you were placed on this earth to do. Speak out about what needs to be spoken. You are valuable. You do matter. You have a Purpose to fulfill. There is Greatness within you.

Speaker Affirmation

"I Speak Loud, I Speak Up, & I Speak Proud Now"
I was quiet too long,
Sometimes in the corner, whispering my song.
Well, God has touched me.
God has set me free.
Time to Speak!
Time to Speak!
Yes, Time to Speak
Out like a bird
Embracing its New Wings.
I'm using my Voice.
Let it Ring, let it Ring.
I said, **Let It, RING!**
No longer bound but I am Free—
Free, Free, Free,

Free to Be,
Free to Be
ME.
THEREFORE
I Speak Loud;
I Speak Up;
I Speak Proud
Now.
I Speak Loud;
I Speak Up;
I Speak Proud
Now.
I Speak Loud;
I Speak Up;
I Speak Proud
Now.
Written by Gladys Peaches Kenney

As I close, let me remind you that this is your Time! No more excuses—someone is interested in hearing the words that you buried alive. Arise and come forth with your VOICE. Today is the beginning of you unleashing what the devil tried to hide because he knew that God was going to use your voice one day. Actually, Today is here. Tell the world what God has shown you. Therefore, **Speak Loud, Speak Up, Speak Proud.**

Motto: ***Coaching You to Step into your Dreams by Faith & Works***

**Cheryl A.S. Hurley** is an extraordinary woman who embraces her life's mission wholeheartedly. A certified Life Coach with a passion for tapping potential and maximizing prospects, she is an expert with over 20 years' experience in creating an open and safe space for individuals to clarify intentions, expand possibilities and reach new heights. Cheryl coaches women to conquer their fears, achieve their dreams and realize their unique purpose despite the circumstances they may have faced.

Born in Philadelphia, Pennsylvania, Cheryl A.S. Hurley has always been a positive influence on her family, friends and colleagues.

Cheryl published her first book, *Empowered, Resilient and Uniquely You!* in September 2017. Her second book, which is co-authored with Pamela Elaine Nichols, *Financial Beauty: 30 Days to an Abundance Mindset* was released in January 2019.

Cheryl is married to Reginald S. Hurley, Sr., has two beautiful children (Reginald Jr. and Shannon) and four adorable grands - Jayden, Trinity, Reginald III and Ryan.

Her Motto: "The legacy that a woman leaves is the one she lives, walks and breathes."

Beating the Odds and Teaching Others to Do the Same

By Cheryl A.S. Hurley

*"Success is to be measured not so much by the position
that one has reached in life as by the obstacles
which he has overcome."*
Booker T. Washington

Born in a section of the city known as 'The Bottom,' I grew up in an era where gang war was prevalent, and I had to travel to and from school with fear. I experienced firsthand brokenness from great adversity in the community, family crises, health challenges, financial struggles and corporate America. I recall hearing many family stories of being extremely sick as a young child and my dad shuffling me back and forth in the snow to the hospital. Upon the discovery of a cyst, I had to undergo surgery at the age of two to have it removed. There was a lot going on which I didn't quite understand as a young child but I recall my mom one day snatching my siblings and me all up and moving in with my grandmom due to my dad's excessive drinking and physical aggression toward her. While he was a loving dad whom we adored, he possessed a level of control over my mom that was frightening.

For much of my growing up years, I watched women in charge, shaking and moving and making things happen. I recall my mother, who worked very hard. She nurtured us and tended to the affairs of efficiently running our household. During it all, including the ongoing tyrants from Dad and our stories to her of his brandishing a gun he said that he was going to harm her with, she became ill from what I am sure was related in some degree to emotional and physical fatigue. As a result, she required surgery and was admitted into the hospital. After undergoing a successful procedure, while recuperating in the hospital, my dad visited her and at her weakest moment physically, he tried to choke the life out of her, which was thankfully thwarted by an orderly who just so happened to come into the room.

As I secretly replayed that event over and over in my head, there was a silent rage that brewed within me, as I simply could not believe that after the many times my siblings and I literally intervened to assure that he would not harm our mother, he chose to go to the hospital to cause her harm. In the midst of my anger I wondered if the need to control another human being could be so strong that one would attempt to violate a person's life all because they could not control their decision-making. While I found this hard to believe, I moved on as if everything was fine when in actuality it wasn't. Yes, I was set apart and chosen but I was covered by the overwhelming, adverse impact of fear and I didn't want to lose my mom.

My grandmother, who was not only the matriarch of our family but also an entrepreneur in her own way, used her gift of domestication to set the standard that created a level of wealth that met her needs as well as the needs of others. When I was 16, she suffered an aneurysm which she succumbed to after a lengthy illness. I watched her tenacious battle during her illness as she had several surgeries, lost her speech and her mobility but was still able to maintain a resilient fortitude. I vividly remember coming home from school and smelling cigarette smoke, which was strange, as no one in our home smoked. As I entered the house, I saw various family members and I knew something was wrong. It was then that I learned that the matriarch – my grand-mother – had passed. I was devastated by the impact of grief.

Beating the Odds by Facing My Giants

I would like to paint a picture of a giant as being 'anything that tries to overshadow your life purpose.' My purpose is to empower, motivate and inspire people. My life experiences brought me before numerous giants. Coupled with some of the earlier experiences I have shared, some of my greatest giants were the pain associated with the death of my father (cancer) and sister (leukemia), financial struggles and after investing 20 years of my life in corporate America, I became aware that my time was undervalued and unappreciated. I soon found myself stuck in the trap of self-pity, the unfairness of life, and the resounding 'why me?' As if that wasn't enough, a boss once informed me that if I could not adjust my thinking and comply with the demands, I could "get the hell out of their facility." My jaw dropped in shock, simply due to the unforeseen turn the conversation had taken. For a moment, I considered whether to park my principles of professionalism and share "my" own personal feelings of the anger brewing inside me or process the adversity I was faced with.

Wisdom won out – I chose to do what I teach – P-R-O-C-E-S-S.

Many people believe they can make a difference; some even believe they can change a nation. We often begin enthusiasti-cally and fully commit to the plan we have in place. However, we do not consider the magnitude of adversity we may face. We are often blindsided by adversity and never see it coming.

For me, just when I thought I was ready to change a nation, I was sidetracked. That's when I found them... uncovered emotions! I was that person who appeared to have everything in control, with no cares in the world. As I write this, I hear an isolated phrase from Patti LaBelle singing, "If only you knew." It was during this moment of uncertainty that I felt the fire was turned up high. I found myself screaming inside during this adverse situation, *When will this ever stop?*

A couple of years ago, I experienced a period of sickness that was extremely scary. I was emotionally in a low place, with a lot of quiet time to reflect on my situation. This quiet time changed my perception of adversity, and a new word was on the horizon. O-P-P-O-R-T-U-N-I-T-Y. This re-ignited "why" I beat the odds and intensified my mission to teach others to do the same.

It was important for me to recall that my early experiences of great adversity equipped me with the opportunities of wisdom and growth that accompanied each obstacle I faced. As soon as I allowed myself to think more clearly, I was able to let go of the self-defeating and toxic thoughts I was harboring and began to see through the lens of opportunity. Never would I have imagined that I would be grateful for experiencing adversity! The lessons I learned through each painful experience equipped me with the necessary tools I needed to beat the odds and prepared me to deal with greater giants. Even though I experienced yet greater giants that were painful, I learned to seek for the lessons to be learned. The greatest lesson I learned was that adversity truly builds character and resilience.

Although adversity is a series of troubles that distract us from attaining goals and finding contentment, and experiences we go through can lead to depression and hopelessness, what's interesting is that everybody – at some point in their lives – will experience adversity. With the right attitude and mindset, and with a refocus on our perception of adversity, it can be overcome.

Re-focus

I have heard many stories of tough times and circumstances from those I have come in contact with. Those anecdotes, coupled with my own experiences, have proven instrumental in my understanding of the power in refocusing our perception of adversity. When faced with adversity, it's easy to become sidetracked by disappointments and obstacles. If we don't refocus our perception of adversity, it can quickly build and become overwhelming. It is during these times that a change in perception of adversity is needed so that we can beat the odds through a new set of lenses known as opportunity.

When a photographer is getting ready to take a picture, he/she will adjust the lens to get a clearer picture. In that same way, we need to adjust our lens as it relates to adversity, so that we let our emotional intelligence guide our perception and behavior.

When faced with adversity, we may often find ourselves stuck in the emotions of the situation. As you are reading this, stop right now to determine and prioritize the challenges keeping you from attaining your purpose. Recognize those things that cause anxiety and give you that sense of hopelessness.

> *"Within the process of birthing your greatness*
> *comes the formidable task of facing the giants*
> *that will attempt to block your path."*
> *TD Jakes*

Beating the Odds and Teaching Others How to do the Same

As we shift our perspective of adversity, we can boldly embrace how it is being used to beat the odds and birth our greatness. One of several tools I have found to gain greater perspective when facing challenges is journaling, which is a form of self-care that allows me to declutter my thoughts through self-expression. When we declutter our mind, we release non-productive thoughts and gain insight into the necessary action steps we need in order to move past the challenges we face. Consider taking intentional reflective moments to journal about ways you can shift your perspective regarding the adversity you may have or are facing to better understand the lesson to be learned as it relates to birthing your personal greatness.

The key – the most important thing to remember – is never to give up! Adversity is always going to be there; the struggle is real, but defeat can be avoided. Do not let outside influences affect the end goal. Rather, use them as opportunities to become a better person. You do matter!

§ Don't stop believing in yourself. Most people have experienced obstacles before.

§ Act upon seeking out a coach or mentor – people who are willing to be supportive and will help you to keep your eyes on the "prize."

§ Come up with a healthy habit such as writing in a gratitude journal. *I am a huge fan of the value found in being grateful. When we develop a grateful attitude, we change our perception of adversity.*

As I often counsel or coach individuals, I am humbly reminded how I beat the odds and overcame obstacles which have become teachable opportunities to help others. It's so easy to look at where you are today without taking a moment to reflect on where you started. What started at the age of two for me has now become what I teach others – there is a purpose in your pain. Our Heavenly Father will take every painful experience and every memory and use them for His good.

Despite the challenging experiences you encounter, I encourage you to remain confident that they mirror the transitional stages in your life that are intentionally being used to birth the seed of greatness that lies within you.

"BREATHE expectantly, LIVE confidently and MOVE Boldly."

The End…but really, the beginning!

You are Set Apart and Chosen! You are an Extraordinary Woman! Walk in this truth.

Blessings,
Kimmoly

Made in the USA
Middletown, DE
10 March 2019